58.00

ST. MATTHEW

The Bible for School and Home

by J. Paterson Smyth

The Book of Genesis

Moses and the Exodus

Joshua and the Judges

The Prophets and Kings

*When the Christ Came:
The Highlands of Galilee*

*When the Christ Came:
The Road to Jerusalem*

St. Matthew

St. Mark

The Bible for School and Home

ST. MATTHEW

by

J. Paterson Smyth

YESTERDAY'S CLASSICS

ITHACA, NEW YORK

This edition, first published in 2017 by Yesterday's Classics, an imprint of Yesterday's Classics, LLC, is an unabridged republication of the text originally published by Sampson Low, Marston & Co., Ltd. For the complete listing of the books that are published by Yesterday's Classics, please visit www.yesterdaysclassics. com. Yesterday's Classics is the publishing arm of the Baldwin Online Children's Literature Project which presents the complete text of hundreds of classic books for children at www.mainlesson.com.

ISBN: 978-1-63334-039-8

Yesterday's Classics, LLC
PO Box 339
Ithaca, NY 14851

CONTENTS

GENERAL INTRODUCTION

I

This series of books is intended for two classes of teachers:

1. *For Teachers in Week Day and Sunday Schools.* For these each book is divided into complete lessons. The lesson will demand preparation. Where feasible there should be diligent use of commentaries and of any books indicated in the notes. *As a general rule* I think the teacher should not bring the book at all to his class if he is capable of doing without it. He should make copious notes of the subject. The lesson should be thoroughly studied and digested beforehand, with all the additional aids at his disposal, and it should come forth at the class warm and fresh from his own heart and brain. But I would lay down no rigid rule about the use of the Lesson Book. To some it may be a burden to keep the details of a long lesson in the memory; and, provided the subject has been very carefully studied, the Lesson Book, with its salient points carefully marked in coloured pencil, may be a considerable help. Let each do what seems best in his particular case, only taking care to satisfy his conscience that it is not done through

laziness, and that he can really do best for his class by the plan which he adopts.

2. *For Parents* who would use it in teaching their children at home. They need only small portions, brief little lessons of about ten minutes each night. For these each chapter is divided into short sections. I should advise that on the first night only the Scripture indicated should be read, with some passing remarks and questions to give a grip of the story. That is enough. Then night after night go on with the teaching, taking as much or as little as one sees fit.

I have not written out the teaching in full as a series of readings which could be read over to the child without effort or thought. With this book in hand a very little preparation and adaptation will enable one to make the lesson more interesting and more personal and to hold the child's attention by questioning. Try to get his interest. Try to make him talk. Make the lesson conversational. Don't preach.

II

HINTS FOR TEACHING

An ancient Roman orator once laid down for his pupils the three-fold aim of a teacher:

1. *Placere* (to interest).

2. *Docere* (to teach).

3. *Movere* (to move).

1. To interest the audience (in order to teach them).

2. To teach them (in order to move them).

3. To move them to action.

On these three words of his I hang a few suggestions on the teaching of this set of Lessons.

1. Placere (to interest)

I want especially to insist on attention to this rule. Some teachers seem to think that to interest the pupils is a minor matter. It is not a minor matter and the pupils will very soon let you know it. Believe me, it is no waste of time to spend hours during the week in planning to excite their interest to the utmost. Most of the complaints of inattention would cease at once if the teacher would give more study to rousing their interest. After all, there is little use in knowing the facts of your subject, and being anxious about the souls of the pupils, if all the time that you are teaching, these pupils are yawning and taking no interest in what you say. I know some have more aptitude for teaching than others. Yet, after considerable experience of teachers whose lesson was a weariness to the flesh, and of teachers who never lost attention for a moment, I am convinced, on the whole, that the power to interest largely depends on the previous preparation.

Therefore do not content yourself with merely studying the teaching of this series. Read widely and freely. Read not only commentaries, but books that will give local interest and colour—books that will throw valuable sidelights on your sketch.

But more than reading is necessary. You know the meaning of the expression, *"Put yourself in his place."* Practise that in every Bible story, using your imagination, living in the scene, experiencing, as far as you can, every feeling of the actors. To some this is no effort at all. They feel their cheeks flushing and their eyes growing moist as they project themselves involuntarily into the scene before them. But though it be easier to some than to others, it is in some degree possible to all, and the interest of the lesson largely depends on it. I have done my best in these books to help the teacher in this respect. But no man can help another much. Success will depend entirely on the effort to "put yourself in his place."

In reading the Bible chapter corresponding to each lesson, I suggest that the teacher should read part of the chapter, rather than let the pupils tire themselves by "reading round." My experience is that this "reading round" is a fruitful source of listlessness. When his verse is read, the pupil can let his mind wander till his turn comes again, and so he loses all interest. I have tried, with success, varying the monotony. I would let them read the first round of verses in order; then I would make them read out of the regular order, as I called their names; and sometimes, if the lesson were long, I would again and again interrupt by reading a group of verses myself, making remarks as I went on. To lose their interest is fatal.

I have indicated also in the lessons that you should not unnecessarily give information yourself. Try to question it *into* them. If you tell them facts which they have just read, they grow weary. If you ask a question, and then answer it yourself when they miss it, you cannot keep their attention. Send your questions around in every sort of order, or want of order. Try to puzzle them—try to surprise them. Vary the form of the question, if not answered, and always feel it to be a defeat if you ultimately fail in getting the answer you want.

2. Docere (to teach)

You interest the pupil in order that you may *teach*. Therefore teach definitely the Lesson that is set you. Do not be content with interesting him. Do not be content either with drawing spiritual teaching. Teach the facts before you. Be sure that God has inspired the narration of them for some good purpose.

When you are dealing with Old Testament characters, do not try to shirk or to condone evil in them. They were not faultless saints. They were men like ourselves, whom God was helping and bearing with, as He helps and bears with us, and the interest of the story largely depends on the pupil realizing this.

In the Old Testament books of this series you will find very full chapters written on the Creation, the Fall, the Flood, the election of Jacob, the Sun standing still, the slaughter of Canaanites, and other such subjects. In connection with these I want to say something that especially concerns teachers. Your pupils, now or later, can hardly avoid coming in contact with the flippant scepticism so common nowadays, which makes jests at the story of the sun standing still, and talks of the folly of believing that all humanity was condemned because Eve ate an apple thousands of years ago. This flippant tone is "in the air." They will meet with it in their companions, in the novels of the day, in popular magazine articles on their tables at home. You have, many of you, met with it yourselves; you know how disturbing it is; and you probably know, too, that much of its influence on people arises from the narrow and unwise teaching of the Bible in their youth. Now you have no right to ignore this in your teaching of the Bible. You need not talk of Bible difficulties and their answers. You need not refer to them at all. But teach the truth that will take the sting out of these difficulties when presented in after-life.

To do this requires trouble and thought. We have learned much in the last fifty years that has thrown new light for us on the meaning of some parts of the Bible; which has, at any rate, made doubtful some of our old interpretations of it. We must not ignore this. There are certain traditional theories which some of us still insist on teaching as God's infallible truth, whereas they are really only human opinions about it, which may possibly be mistaken. As long as they are taught as human opinions, even if we are wrong, the mistake will do no harm. But if things are taught as God's infallible truth, to be believed on peril of doubting God's Word, it may do grave mischief, if in after-life the pupil find them seriously disputed, or perhaps false. A shallow, unthinking man, finding part of his teaching false, which has been associated in his mind with the most solemn sanctions of religion, is in danger of letting the whole go. Thus many of our young people drift into hazy doubt about the Bible. Then we get troubled about their beliefs, and give them books of Christian evidences to win them back by explaining that what was taught them in childhood was not *quite* correct, and needs now to be modified by a broader and slightly different view. But we go on as before with the younger generation, and expose them in their turn to the same difficulties.

Does it not strike you that, instead of this continual planning to win men back from unbelief, it might be worth while to try the other method of not exposing them to unbelief? Give them the more careful and intelligent teaching at first, and so prepare them to meet the difficulties by-and-by.

I have no wish to advocate any so-called "advanced" teaching. Much of such teaching I gravely object to. But there are truths of which there is no question amongst thoughtful people, which somehow are very seldom taught to the young, though ignorance about them in after-life leads to grave doubt and misunderstanding. Take, for example, the gradual, progressive nature of God's teaching in Scripture, which makes the Old Testament teaching as a whole lower than that of the New. This is certainly no doubtful question, and the knowledge of it is necessary for an intelligent study of

Scripture. I have dealt with it where necessary in some of the books of this series.

I think, too, our teaching on what may seem to us doubtful questions should be more fearless and candid. If there are two different views each held by able and devout men, do not teach your own as the infallibly true one, and ignore or condemn the other. For example, do not insist that the order of creation must be accurately given in the first chapter of Genesis. You may think so; but many great scholars, with as deep a reverence for the Bible as you have, think that inspired writers were circumscribed by the science of their time. Do not be too positive that the story of the Fall *must be* an exactly literal narrative of facts. If you believe that it is I suppose you must tell your pupil so. But do not be afraid to tell him also that there are good and holy and scholarly men who think of it as a great old-world allegory, like the parable of the Prodigal Son, to teach in easy popular form profound lessons about sin. Endeavor in your Bible teaching "to be thoroughly truthful: to assert nothing as certain which is not certain, nothing as probable which is not probable, and nothing as more probable than it is." Let the pupil see that there are some things that we cannot be quite sure about, and let him gather insensibly from your teaching the conviction that truth, above all things, is to be loved and sought, and that religion has never anything to fear from discovering the truth. If we could but get this healthy, manly, common-sense attitude adopted now in teaching the Bible to young people, we should, with

God's blessing, have in the new generation a stronger and more intelligent faith.

3. Movere (to move)

All your teaching is useless unless it have this object: to move the heart, to rouse the affections toward the love of God, and the will toward the effort after the blessed life. You interest in order to teach. You teach in order to move. *That* is the supreme object. Here the teacher must be left largely to his own resources. One suggestion I offer: don't preach. At any rate, don't preach much lest you lose grip of your pupils. You have their attention all right while their minds are occupied by a carefully prepared lesson; but wait till you close your Bible, and, assuming a long face, begin, "And now, boys," etc. and straightway they know what is coming, and you have lost them in a moment.

Do not change your tone at the application of your lesson. Try to keep the teaching still conversational. Try still in this more spiritual part of your teaching to question into them what you want them to learn. Appeal to the judgment and to the conscience. I can scarce give a better example than that of our Lord in teaching the parable of the Good Samaritan. He first interested His pupil by putting His lesson in an attractive form, and then He did not append to it a long, tedious moral. He simply asked the man before Him, "Which of these three *thinkest thou?*"—i.e., "What do you think about it?" The interest was still kept up. The man, pleased at the appeal to his judgment, replied promptly, "He that showed mercy on him;" and on the instant came the quick rejoinder, "Go, and do thou likewise." Thus the lesson ends. Try to work on that model.

Now, while forbidding preaching to your pupils, may I be permitted a little preaching myself? This series of lessons is intended for Sunday schools as well as week-day schools. It is of Sunday-school teachers I am thinking in what I am now about to say. I cannot escape the solemn feeling of the responsibility of every teacher for the children in his care. Some of these children have little or no religious influence exerted on them for the whole week except in this one hour with you. Do not make light of this work. Do not get to think, with good-natured optimism, that all the nice, pleasant children in your class are pretty sure to be Christ's soldiers and servants by-and-by. Alas! for the crowds of these nice, pleasant children, who, in later life, wander away from Christ into the ranks of evil. Do not take this danger lightly. Be anxious; be prayerful; be terribly in earnest, that the one hour in the week given you to use be wisely and faithfully used.

But, on the other hand, be very hopeful too, because of the love of God. He will not judge you hardly. Remember that He will bless very feeble work, if it be your best. Remember that He cares infinitely more for the children's welfare than you do, and, therefore, by His grace, much of the teaching about which you are despondent may bring forth good fruit in the days to come. Do you know the lines about "The Noisy Seven"?—

"I wonder if he remembers—
 Our sainted teacher in heaven—
The class in the old grey schoolhouse,
 Known as the 'Noisy Seven'?

"I wonder if he remembers
 How restless we used to be.
Or thinks we forget the lesson
 Of Christ and Gethsemane?

"I wish I could tell the story
 As he used to tell it then;
I'm sure that, with Heaven's blessing,
 It would reach the hearts of men.

"I often wish I could tell him,
 Though we caused him so much pain
By our thoughtless, boyish frolic,
 His lessons were not in vain.

"I'd like to tell him how Willie,
 The merriest of us all,
From the field of Balaclava
 Went home at the Master's call.

"I'd like to tell him how Ronald,
 So brimming with mirth and fun,
Now tells the heathen of India
 The tale of the Crucified One.

"I'd like to tell him how Robert,
 And Jamie, and George, and 'Ray,'
Are honoured in the Church of God—
 The foremost men of their day.

"I'd like, yes, I'd like to tell him
    What his lesson did for me;
And how I am trying to follow
    The Christ of Gethsemane.

"Perhaps he knows it already,
    For Willie has told him, maybe,
That we are all coming, coming
    Through Christ of Gethsemane.

"How many besides I know not
    Will gather at last in heaven,
The fruit of that faithful sowing,
    But the sheaves are already seven."

INTRODUCTION TO ST. MATTHEW

Two thoughts have been prominent in writing these Lessons on St. Matthew's Gospel. It may be well to indicate them here.

I

The first is the thought of Christ's "Kingdom of God" as a sort of colony of Heaven down here on earth. A leading idea of ancient Rome was that of the founding of colonies throughout the world, whose laws should be the laws of Rome, and whose citizens should have the same duties and privileges as the citizens of the Imperial City. An idea something like this runs through the New Testament references to the founding of the "Kingdom of God," and especially in St. Matthew's Gospel, which is preëminently the "Gospel of the Kingdom." These Lessons on St. Matthew are, therefore, written with the central thought that our Lord's aim for His "Kingdom" was that it should be a sort of "colony" of Heaven to be founded on earth—a colony whose laws should be the laws of Heaven, whose subjects should be obedient to the authority of Heaven's King; and whose future should be in the perfect Kingdom of Heaven above.

Try to carry on this thought, which will be suggested

to you all through by the titles of the Lessons. The children can easily be taught to get hold of it. Think of the Roman colony at Philippi, whose citizens so identified themselves with the far-off Imperial City, rejecting "customs not lawful for us to receive or to observe, being Romans" (Acts xvi. 21). Think of St. Paul's teaching about the colony of the Kingdom of Heaven to these same Philippians, so proud of being citizens of Imperial Rome—"Our citizenship is in Heaven" (Philippians iii. 20, R.V.). Try to press on the children this thought of the Kingdom of God on earth as a colony of Heaven. There are "customs not lawful for us to receive or observe, being members of the Kingdom of God." Try to teach them the real, practical religion implied in being members of that Kingdom. The thought is worked out more fully in Lesson III.

II

The second thought is this: that in order that the children may learn to love and trust our blessed Lord, it is above all things necessary that they should get to KNOW HIM; to become acquainted with Him in the same sense as one gets to know and become acquainted with a human friend. It is little use to tell them of the *duty* of loving or trusting Him. We can never love or trust anybody as a duty. We have learned to trust our dearest friends simply by *knowing* them, by letting their character reveal itself till we could no longer withhold our trust. That is the only way of learning to love or trust anybody, God or man.

Therefore must it be the prominent object in

teaching the Gospel story that the child should insensibly be "acquainting himself with God," learning God's character, getting into touch with the heart of Jesus Christ. The events of the history, however interesting, must never obscure this. The purpose of every lesson must be to show His tenderness, His unselfishness, His patience, His love; taking care, in the proper places, to emphasize also His sterner side: His anger at hypocrisy; His indignant championship of the little ones; His sensitiveness to pain, and yet His calm courage in facing pain for others' sake.

Do not worry the child with demands for admiration of these qualities. Do not keep telling him that he ought to love and admire, etc. Only pray for grace to present the Christ-character aright. Have faith in the power of that character to win all you desire.

Which of us has not often prayed for more love and trust in Christ, and more enthusiasm about Him? We know that we could love—aye, love enthusiastically— such a man if He lived in our midst to-day, and IF WE KNEW HIM intimately, as we know our closest friend. Therefore, surely, the highest thing we can do for the children is to help them to *know* Him while their hearts are young and susceptible. It is the only thing that matters much—thus knowing Christ. It is good to know obscure prophecies, and understand Bible difficulties, and good to have clear views about many theological dogmas; but all are of minor importance to the great object of the study of the Bible—to "KNOW THEE, the only true God, and Jesus Christ, whom Thou hast sent."

THE COMING OF THE KING

St. Matthew I. 18 to end, and II.

Take care to begin solemnly with the thought of Christ's Godhead and pre-existence. Divide the Lesson, for clearness, into four sections, as indicated. Show the class in Bible that section i. 18-25, is about the Miraculous Birth; the next (ii. 1-12) about visit of Wise Men; and so on.

§ 1. The Preparation

The most interesting and wonderful story in the world. But to keep up its interest and its wonder, two things are necessary. (1) We must exert our imaginations to picture vividly the scenes, and try to live in them, as it were, so as to escape the deadness which comes from knowing the story already. But also (2) we must take care in our vivid picturing not to become too familiar, not to think of "the Boy Jesus" as lightly as we should think of a boy in the next street. Must remind ourselves of His being God, and of solemn meaning of the Miraculous Birth—God becoming manifest in the flesh.

If writing your life, what first? Birth. Yes, that is beginning of you. Is that so of our Lord? (John xvii. 5.) Millions of ages before the world was—so far back that brain reels at the thought—still He was there. He was God. Was He at Creation? John i. 1-3. And at the sad Fall which we thought of recently? Was He sorry? Then began His promises that He would come and help up the poor world again. First promise? Genesis iii. 15. Explain. Then tell me any of the promises to Abraham which we had lately? (Genesis xii. 2, 3; xxii. 15-18; xxviii. 14; etc.); to David? (Psalms ii. 6; xlv. 3, 4; lxii.); to Isaiah? (ix. 6, 7; xxxii. 1); to other prophets? (Jeremiah xxiii. 5, 6; Micah v. 2-5; Daniel ii. 44; Zechariah ix. 9; etc.) Only time just to remind of them. So for thousands of years the world went on, and still He did not come. But the world was waiting. And God was preparing all the time, watching the world, getting all things ready. At last "fulness of time come" (Galatians iv. 4), when our story to-day begins. All the separate little nations welded into one great Roman empire, with its one language; with its splendid roads reaching everywhere from Rome; with the people getting worse and more in need of the Christ. Everything ready for founding of His Kingdom. And people seemed to feel that the King must be coming. Everywhere amongst the Jews an excited expectancy. (See Luke ii. 25, 26, 38; Acts xxvi. 7; etc.) And even some of the learned heathen, too, looking forward in a puzzled way to the coming of some great One. Then opens St. Matthew's story in ch. i. 18-25, told to emphasize that Christ was not of human birth.

§ 2. The Miraculous Coming

Simple, beautiful story. A betrothed couple in country village of Nazareth. Ever see village carpenter's shop? Where? Describe? Like that, a village workshop in the Nazareth street, and a strong, broad-shouldered carpenter working at his bench with saw and hammer and chisel, making tables and chairs, and ploughs and cattle-yokes for the country-people. Working hard and joyfully to prepare a new home. Why? Engaged to be married soon. To whom? Living in other end of village with her mother, working in the house, making bread, and spinning, and drawing water from the well with other village girls in the evenings. Don't you think she was very beautiful? At any rate, surely beautiful in soul, gentle and modest, loving and religious.

And Joseph the carpenter loved her dearly. I think he was older than she was, and he was very tender to her, and liked to watch her passing, and liked to think of the little home he was making for her. And it must have been pleasant to her to meet him, and to hear him talk of all his brave hopes and plans for their future. I think, too, they cared so much for religion, that they often talked of God's promise of the Messiah. And I can imagine the girl going home after her talks, and kneeling down at her bedside to pray for God's blessing on her lover's life and her own. Little she dreamed how wonderful would be the answer.

Then came a day that she could never forget.

One day, just before St. Matthew's story begins—perhaps at prayer—suddenly a wonderful visitor. Who?

(Luke i. 26.) What did he announce? Think of the awe, and astonishment, and trembling joy. She to be the mother of the Messiah that all the nation hoped for. Fancy her excitement! Wanting to tell someone. Whom did she tell? (Luke i. 39.) Perhaps angel did not wish her to tell Joseph, and that she had to carry her secret in her own wondering heart, only talking of it to God in her prayers. By-and-by God revealed it to Joseph. How? Very joyful and comforting, but surely very solemn too. Messiah coming. Emmanuel—God with us. And this stupendous miracle should be through his affianced wife. He was to take her home, and live in reverent awe with her, and be God's guardian for the little Child when born. What was he to call Him? Why? (v. 21.) Yes. Not merely save from pain, or unhappiness, or hell-fire—that, too—but, most important of all, "from their sins." With God that is more important than all the rest. Therefore, how can one know whether he is being saved by Lord Jesus? If he sees that he is getting help to conquer meanness, and selfishness, and badness of every kind, and to grow noble, and strong, and unselfish, and lovable—then he sees he is being saved. That is God's meaning of salvation. Will He do that for anybody who comes? That was what He came for. "Him that cometh unto Me I will in no wise cast out."

You remember St. Luke's story of the birth-day of our Lord (Luke ii.). Angels again. It seems heaven so overflowing with joyful excitement that the angels could not keep still. Joy for what? God's generous love to poor men and women who had sinned. Do angels care? (Luke xv. 10.) I suppose these angels had seen the

Creation, and grieved over Fall; and then watched and waited all these centuries, never growing older. Now the joy of telling of God's generous goodness to the shepherds watching in the fields.

§ 3. *The Wise Men from the East*

Some other people watching hundreds of miles away in the East that night? Perhaps in Daniel's far-off land of Chaldea. "Wise Men," magi—astronomers, like Daniel. What did they see? We really know nothing further about this star; must have been some miraculous light low down, since no ordinary star could point out a house. All we know is that God in some way taught these wise astronomers about the coming Messiah, and then, since they were eager to find Him, guided them by this star. Perhaps they lived in Daniel's country, or Balaam's country, and knew their prophecies; or, perhaps, Jews living there told them of expected Messiah.

At any rate, they heard of Him, and were eager to find Him; and so God revealed, as He always does to eager souls, how to find Him. They were heathens, Gentiles—not Jews. Is it not nice to learn that God was teaching heathens and Gentiles, while the Jews thought He only cared for themselves? The Jews always thought that. In Old Testament they thought that God cared nothing about Canaanites or Ninevites, or any heathen. Yet you remember. God had Melchizedek amongst Canaanites; and Jethro, and Balaam, and Job, and Jonah were His teachers of religion to other heathen races. Christian people sometimes think like Jews; but it is wrong. God is Father of all—Christ is Brother of all; and "in every nation he that feareth God and worketh righteousness is acceptable unto Him." That is why God is so desirous that we should bring the light of Gospel to the poor heathen, whom He is watching over with as much care as He watches over us.

So they came. Away, away, over mountains and deserts, on their camels, with the rich, barbaric trappings, and bearing their costly gifts. Remember pictures of them on Christmas cards—three kings: Gaspar, Melchior, Balthazar. Cologne Cathedral claims to have their tombs and their skulls; but really nobody knows anything of them except what this chapter tells. At last, after long weeks or months, they arrive at Jerusalem. Imagine them, with their jingling trappings and foreign appearance, riding in and asking everyone they met—what? I suppose they expected to see banners, and rejoicing, and illuminations everywhere, and all men talking of the young king. Was it so? No; though they had the prophecies of Scripture, and professed to expect Him, no one seemed to care. Like many to-day. Imagine poor blacks coming eagerly to you, as you leave Sunday school to-day, asking you about the good news of Christ. Should you tell them with joy, or should you be puzzled or indifferent? Why so? Is not there good news about Christ? Do you know it? Are you glad? These Jerusalem Bible-readers stared, and wondered, and chattered, and crowded around the strangers till they must have grown quite discouraged about their quest. At last Herod, in his white palace, heard of it. Was he glad? Why? What did he do? What did the priests and scribes tell him? What prophet wrote it? Then Herod thought of a very clever, crooked trick. What? Wise men, not accustomed to meanness and scheming, did not see the trick; thought Herod a very good, kind king. What questions did he ask? Why? So he sent them away with kind words, and they promised what? What was his object? What an utter fool that old king was! What a fool everybody is who tries to oppose God! Could all the kings of the world put together do it? Like so many little children opposing an express train.

Tell me rest of the story of the Wise Men. Yes. God guided them, and rewarded all their faith and all their exertions; and they found the Lord Jesus, and worshipped Him. That is always result of earnest seeking. How did they show their devotion to Him? Yes. Gave Him the best and costliest things they had. They were the first Gentiles who found the Lord. We are the later Gentiles finding Him. How must we show our devotion? Same way. Offer what? The best we have—of money, of brains, of strength, of influence, etc. No real worship of Him except thus. All else is mockery. On what Church festival do we celebrate this visit of Wise Men?

§ 4. *The Holy Innocents*

How did Herod's trick succeed? (ii. 12.) Was he vexed? Yes, and frightened. Thought they must be plotting for the new king. But he thought of another way to destroy Christ? Yes. Fancy the officer getting such a brutal order—how he would hate the old tyrant who had already killed his own queen and three sons. Yet he obeyed; called out the soldiers, and sent them to Bethlehem.

Think of the little village children running to meet them, and looking at their gay dresses and beautiful horses. Surely some of the soldiers must have hated the terrible task. That night the whole village was in uproar—mothers shrieking and grappling with the murderers, and the poor little dead and dying boys[1] lying in the streets. And little use it was to that cruel old wretch who ordered it to save his throne. For the Babe Jesus was safe, in spite of it all. Where? How? And in a few weeks Herod was dead himself, and summoned before his God. He thought himself wise and clever. Was he? Was it worth while doing all this wickedness? Is it ever worth while doing wickedness? What would have been the truest wisdom for Herod? To follow the little promptings of good that God sends to all men, even to him—to try to be unselfish and loving, and make others happy, and never mind about himself or his throne. That is always the truest wisdom. Always keep "never minding" about yourself, and following highest and most unselfish instincts. Then you are surely on God's side, and all will be well.

Think of the poor little boys—the first who ever died for Jesus' sake. They did not know; but surely God did not on that account let them lose by it. There is a beautiful picture of the Triumph of the Innocents,

[1](*Ch.* ii. 16.) All the "*male* children" (*see* R.V.). So the massacre would not be a very great one. Not many boys under two in Bethlehem.

where these little children of Bethlehem, after their death, are pictured, wreathed and twined in beautiful flowers, crowding round the Child Jesus as he was carried away into Egypt; and Jesus is stretching out His little hands to them in glad, loving welcome. It is only a painter's fancy. But it teaches surely what is true of every child who dies for the Lord Jesus, like the poor black boys in Uganda a few years since, and of every child, too, who lives for Jesus, as you, I trust, are going to do.

HOW THE KING WAS CROWNED, AND WENT FORTH TO BATTLE

St. Matthew III. and IV. to v. 12.

§ 1. Childhood and Youth

Remind briefly of last Sunday's story. How old was the Lord Jesus then? How old in to-day's story? (Luke iii. 23.) Notice briefly what happened meantime. How the little Child grew up, child-like, natural, like the others, only more brave and unselfish and lovable. How He played with the other village children in the market-place. When He was a grown man, He thinks of one of the old games—a sort of "weddings and funerals" game (Matthew xi. 16, 17). How He was obedient and helpful at home (Luke ii. 51). How He went to village school, and sat on the floor with all the others, and learned whole pages of the Bible by heart. That was the usual lesson-book. Interesting scene in Longfellow's *Golden Legend*, the Rabbi ben-Israel's school:—

"Come hither, Judas Iscariot,
Say if thy lesson thou hast got

. . .

Now little Jesus, the carpenter's Son,
Let us see how Thy task is done," etc.

How at twelve years old He went up to Passover (Luke ii. 42), probably met His cousin John, and sat with him at Passover feast, where the youngest child—perhaps Himself—had to say the words, "What mean ye by this service?" and the oldest man arose to explain "It is the sacrifice of the Lord's Passover," etc. (Exodus xii. 27). Don't you think great thoughts would begin to stir in the Child as He wondered about that Passover, which for all these centuries had pointed to Himself—as He saw the Holy City and the white-robed priests and choir-boys, and bowed low in the grand cathedral worship of the Temple? How He came back and was bound to Joseph's trade; and when Joseph died, He had to support His widowed mother, and became known as "Jesus the carpenter," to whom the country-people came to buy chairs and boxes and cattle-yokes, as they did to Joseph before. I like to think of His having to work, and buy, and sell, like ordinary men, making all work and trade holy. But all the while the great thoughts were deepening—the Divine passion for helping others and sacrificing Himself. How troubled and perplexed He would be about the sick and cripples, and especially the wicked—cruel, selfish boys, and girls, and men!

And the clergy and teachers not much good. Not teaching love and self-sacrifice, but mumbling old, tedious rules, and fighting over little theological differences, and "not touching with one of their fingers" the people's burdens of body, and heart, and brain. I can fancy all the pain in His heart, and the furrows on His face, as He got older. I can fancy the lonely boy stealing out at night into the hills to unburden His heart, and pray for God's blessing on the poor world, and how Mary would wonder as she saw Him come in with the strange, earnest light in his eyes.

But He had to restrain Himself till his time was come that He should go forth to help for all eternity the world's troubles, by founding His "Kingdom of God" for the blessing of men.

§ 2. *The Herald of the King*

Now we come to story of to-day. Jesus is thirty years old, and all the country is ringing with the rumour about his cousin John. The Nazareth people coming to the workshop can talk of nothing else. "A great prophet." "Elijah come back." "All the people crowding to him," etc. For hundreds of years no prophet. No wonder they ask: "Is God coming back as of old?" "Is Messiah coming?" "Why this prophet now?" Could you answer them? (Luke i. 76.) What prophecy did John quote? (Matthew iii. 3.) He was to prepare the way for Christ—the voice crying before the King, like the Eastern herald that ran before the royal procession, calling out, "The King! the King!"

Our Lord must have felt now that He can stay no longer. His time is come. Patiently for thirty years He had waited. Now the Divine longing must have its way. He must go out to lift up the poor world. So one day, in His simple dress, He suddenly appears in the crowd listening to John at Jordan. Describe scene before Him. What was John like? The crowd? Listening, do you think? Ah! they had to listen there. Whenever a great soul like that, full of enthusiasm for his message, thinking not of advancement or praise, or fine clothes, giving up everything in his eager excitement to rouse men to righteousness—people can't help listening. What else were they doing? (*v.* 6.) How our Lord's heart must have been throbbing as He watched the preacher! Very gentle preacher, was he? Some of the great rulers and teachers came. Did he speak more gently to them because they were great people? (*v.* 7.) Did he turn them off? No. But insists on what? (*v.* 8.) Yes; righteousness, reality. No talk about their feelings or religious notions, nor their belonging to Jewish Church. No, said John, the righteous life is the one supreme thing. Be real, be earnest, be true. Bring forth good fruit, or else what? Don't you think John was an awkward sort of preacher for hypocrites, and humbugs, and sentimental talkers about religion?

John's two great subjects? (*vv.* 2, 3.) (1) Repent; (2) The Kingdom of Heaven is at hand. Meaning of Kingdom of Heaven we shall see in next Lesson. But a kingdom at any rate must have a king. Whom? So the whole of John's sermon led up to proclaiming the King. How? (*vv.* 11, 12.) And the mighty prophet-preacher, so stern and high in his tone to the great people of earth, bows lowly and humble as he thinks about the coming King, "the latchet of whose shoes I am not worthy to unloose" (Luke iii. 16). And show how humbly he compares his own gifts and power of helping people with those of Christ (*v.* 11).

All this time Jesus was in the crowd, quietly awaiting His turn, standing in his simple country dress by the river. Now He comes down. Did He come confessing His sins, like the rest? Why not? What did John say? Do you think John knew Him to be the Christ? (John i. 33.) But he knew his cousin as the truest noblest heart on earth, in whom no man had ever seen meanness, or selfishness, or any sin. So felt unworthy to baptize Him. Now tell me of baptism, and the wonderful event, the crowning of the King from Heaven? Did the crowd see it? We don't know. Did John? (John i. 33.) Astonished, struck dumb with reverence and awe, he saw his young carpenter cousin claimed as God. Like as if, when Peter the Great was working in an English dockyard in disguise, the Court of Russia should suddenly appear and crown him amid his workmen-companions. That is why I call this "the Crowning of the King," as His great life-work began. Began with a battle.

§ 3. *The Battle and Victory*

Evening come. Crowd departed. John has retired to his cave in awe and wonder. And Jesus departed, too, alone. Where? Away, away out into wild desert country. Could not rest. Great thoughts and yearnings stirring in His soul. His whole life stirred to its foundation by this wondrous scene. The Spirit of God pressing powerfully on Him. He must be away, alone in communion with

His Father. Away, away through the starry night, into the trackless desert, not thinking of danger, nor of the wild beasts, nor of hunger, nor of anything, but the great, wonderful thoughts that are filling His soul. And so rapt is He in His great future, and His communion with God, and His delight in the self-sacrifice for men, that He forgets even to eat—for how long? People in great mental excitement often forget hunger and pain for a time.

But when excitement over, there comes terrible reaction; feels weak, and tired, and despondent. Very hard time to resist temptation. This time, therefore, chosen by Satan for his most powerful attacks. Why attack Christ? If he can make Him sin, it will spoil His power. Whether Satan came as a great black angel of evil, or whether visible at all, we don't know. Do you remember story of his first coming to man? (Genesis iii.) Did he ever come to you? Visible? How? Perhaps like that to Jesus. We don't know. Perhaps St. Matthew did not know. Who must have given account of the Temptation? Why? Because no one else knew but He. And whether the tempter visible or not, Christ says he was the devil. Think of this when you feel him tempting you. A great, real, wicked devil. Don't say, "I feel bad desires and thoughts," but say, "I am tempted of the devil," like our Lord, and rise up and fight him bravely in the strength which our Lord will give you.

Remember, too, Jesus had to fight him *as a man.* He had "emptied Himself." There would have been no need to show that as God He could triumph over Satan. But He had come down to our level as our brother, and would take no advantage that we could not have. Like an armoured knight of old, fighting in front of his peasant soldiers, but putting away his armour, and shield, and horse, and fighting just as they, to inspirit them.

What was the first temptation? Could He do it? Was it a sore temptation? What harm would it have been? Because He was our brother, must fight like His brothers, and trust in God. Never use for His own gain the Divine power. Would be like the knight, when in danger, saving himself by putting on his armour, which his poor brethren could not have. No, He would trust in God; and into his mind at once flashed a verse, which perhaps He had learned in the old rabbi's village school. What was it? "Man shall not," etc. Good thing in temptation to know one's Bible. Then Satan, seeing His trust, very cunningly tries to tempt him that way.

Second temptation? Yes. "Trust God to keep you if you throw yourself off temple." Why should not He? Because it is only in the path of duty we may trust God. If anything be your duty, do it, even at risk of life, and trust God. But not if go into needless danger, doing your own will, to win admiration or recognition from others. What text quoted.

Third temptation? I don't quite understand how this could be a temptation. What did Jesus care about earthly glory, and money, and power? Perhaps this was a stupid blunder of Satan. He was very cunning and subtle; but low, degraded souls cannot understand high and noble souls. Very cunning, tricky, self-seeking man, who could "buy and sell" the wisest around him, yet would be quite unable to understand an utterly noble, unselfish man, full of enthusiasm for God and self-sacrifice. And so would not know how to tempt such a one. Perhaps it was that. Or perhaps he thought Jesus so anxious to get the kingdoms to bless them, that He would be willing to "do evil that good might come." Would He? What was the third answer from Scripture?

Then what happened? (*v.* 11.) Battle over, victory won. Did it ever happen with you? Try to make it happen, and you will learn that the devil is a bully and a coward. Like a bully at school, squaring up to a small boy to frighten him; but if small boy hits back, the bully runs away. So Satan (James iv. 7). It is a great delight to drive him off, one feels so glad, and proud, and thankful. Especially remember that the devil *leaves* us. He is not omnipresent, any more than omnipotent. Some think he is, and they lose heart in temptation, and say: "I may as well give in now as later, for this strain of temptation will be always pressing on me." It is not so. The time of your sharpest temptation is "his hour and the power of darkness." Remember that. Fight through it. And perhaps it will be days and days before a really fierce temptation comes again. Try it next time, and you will see how beautifully all our Lord's fight was for your encouragement and example. The devil will leave you, and in the comfort and peace you will feel as if angels were come to minister unto you.

THE KINGDOM AND ITS LAWS

St. Matthew IV. 12 to end, and V. to v. 27.

I have written a very full Lesson. Teach what you can of it. Don't waste a moment. Don't preach. Keep up interest by lively questioning. It is a most important Lesson, and worth a whole week's trouble to get in touch with it. Especially teach the idea of the Kingdom. St. Matthew's is especially "the Gospel of the Kingdom."

Indicate that iv. 12, is beginning of our Lord's public ministry; but before it occurred the events in John i. to iii. 24, for then (iii. 24) "John was not yet cast into prison." Therefore show from those events that Jesus and some of the disciples called (Matthew iv. 18) were already acquaintances.

§ 1. *The Kingdom of God*

Tell me the titles of the last two Lessons? What were they about? Who was the King? In order to be a king one must have what? A kingdom. Now I want you to be clear about that kingdom, the great ideal ever present to our Lord's mind. What was John the Baptist's first text when preparing the way for our Lord? (*ch.* iii. 2.) And what our Lord's first text? (iv. 17.) So the very first thing He taught was about a kingdom. Now, what was the very last thing He taught? (Acts i. 3.) And if you look through Concordance, you will find the expression "Kingdom of God," or "Kingdom of Heaven," about a hundred times: e.g., Mark i. 15; Luke iv. 43; viii. 10; ix. 2; etc. He was always talking about it in some form. It was the central point of all His teaching, the vision that filled up His enthusiastic outlook into the future.

You know how every human teacher who is capable of excitement and enthusiasm about his work has some special pet subject—temperance, or missions, or hospitals, or child-rescue, or the housing of the poor, etc.—about which he is always wanting to rouse people. Every conversation, every speech of his, somehow leads into it, till people say at last, "Well, that man has temperance, or missions, etc., on the brain. He can't talk of anything else." So we may reverently say of our Lord, His central subject, His great enthusiasm, was the founding on earth of what he called THE KINGDOM OF GOD. For that He lived, and taught, and suffered, and died. For that He enlisted His followers, and told them to enlist others. For that everything was done.

Now, what did He mean by the Kingdom of God? Heaven, you say—a happy place to go to when we die. Did He mean that? No, He did not. At least that was only part—the far-off and final part—of His plan. Whatever He meant, it was clearly something that first of all concerned this earth; that had to begin, and grow, and spread for a blessing on earth. How do we know? Remember parables about it? What was it like? Little mustard seed growing to be a great tree—little bit of leaven spreading in a large quantity of meal—little corn of wheat springing gradually up—the blade, the ear, the full corn in the ear. Would that mean heaven? Evidently He meant some living, growing thing, spreading gradually *on earth*, for earth's blessing and good. He put this beyond all question in the prayer of the kingdom which He taught His followers to use. What? "Thy Kingdom come, Thy will be done"—where? ON EARTH! "on earth, as it is in heaven." Not a prayer for the far future, or for a land beyond the sky, but that now, and here, in school, and home, and office, and shop, the Kingdom of God should come. (Read what is said about "colony of Heaven," in Introduction.)

§ 2. The Ideal of the Kingdom

Let me reverently try to picture what I think was in His mind when He thought with glad hope and enthusiasm about the success of His plan. Try and make the picture in your minds as I go on. He sees before Him a sweet, fair vision—a band of boys and girls, and men and women, of true, noble, generous, Christ-like hearts; the sort of people that you can't help loving and admiring; the sort of people that make life so happy and lovely for all around them. Do you know any person like that? It is a small band at first—small, like a grain of mustard seed—only about twenty or thirty, but growing, growing, as the ages go on, till it overspreads the face of

35

the earth. He sees in the vision how everything bad and miserable vanishes before them—all greediness, and lying, and bullying, and spite, and drunkenness, and impurity; all selfishness and cruelty; all poverty, and misery, and pain. They are such brave, generous boys; such tender, unselfish girls; such noble, self-sacrificing men and women, in some degree like the Lord Himself. They care for nothing but what is good and true. They fear nothing but grieving their King. Their chief thought is the service of the Kingdom—making all life around them happy, and holy, and beautiful. Would not it be lovely to see a great, growing band like that, increasing every day? Would not they make this a happy, holy, beautiful world? Would not they watch over the sick, help the drunkard, and comfort the sorrowful? Do you think the mean, sneaking sort of boys would dare to be mean and sneaking? Would not the spiteful, and untruthful, and selfish girls be utterly ashamed of themselves? Would not many people want to join the ranks of this Kingdom of God, if they saw it so grand, so beautiful, so lovable, spreading over the earth? Well, that is, I think, the vision of our Lord. That is what He meant by the Kingdom of God. Which should begin where? On earth; and go on whither? To Heaven. How do people join the Kingdom? Baptism. Are you a member? What, then, is your duty as a member? (Be earnest over this. Don't be content till you have tried your best to rouse each child to Christ's beautiful ideal for him.)

§ 3. The Founding of the Kingdom

How did He begin to found His Kingdom? By
getting soldiers, and cannons, and swords to fight, as
earthly kings do? No. His Kingdom not like that. You
know now what He wanted done in the world; how
would you begin if you wanted it done? He began by
preaching about it (*vv.* 17 and 23), then by gathering
together a few earnest, unselfish men and women,
and boys and girls, and inspiring them with His own
eagerness and enthusiasm for serving others.

Tell me the first of His new members (*vv.* 18-22.)
Were they strangers to Him? (John i. 40, etc.) He had
already made friends with them; they knew Him,
and were in sympathy with Him, and were probably
expecting this call some day to start at making the new
Kingdom to bless the world. Very few. How was it like
leaven, and corn, and grain of mustard seed? But more
and more disciples came as they heard Him, and saw the
wonderful miracles. Tell me some of the miracles? At last
time came for a solemn founding of the new Kingdom.
St. Luke tells more fully than St. Matthew—what? (Luke
vi. 12-26.) Climbed up the mountain one evening, and
there all night long, alone under the starry sky, kept
praying to His Father, and thinking of His glorious plan
for the world. All night long alone, and then in the early
morning, with the earnest light in His eyes, and great
solemn purpose in His heart, He came down to a level
place on the mountain-side. Crowds waiting, disciples
waiting quietly, solemnly, as He came. Then He told the
whole band of disciples that He was about to choose
twelve Apostles out of them to be the chief helpers in

the new Kingdom. Imagine the breathless waiting to see whom He would choose. Imagine school captain of football team choosing players for a big match. Only this match was to be against the devil, and all the misery and sin of life. One by one he called the names, each wondering who would be called next. Peter! Andrew! John! James! etc. One by one they rose and came. How solemnly the crowd would watch. One of the greatest days in the history of the world.

§ 4. *The Laws of the Kingdom*

Now the Kingdom of God begun. And then solemnly the King begins to tell its laws. Remember similar scene in Old Testament. There God awful in lightnings and thunders. Here God in form of man, sitting as comrade beside them. Note the kindly form of the laws: all blessings. Note, too, that they are, not a *command to do* something, but a *description of character*, which should be the character of the members of His new Kingdom. Note also that it is not each precept alone, but a*ll together*, that form that character. Therefore we must think of them connectedly. Now listen to the Laws of the Kingdom for the Apostles and disciples, and you and me, and all Christians.

1. POOR IN SPIRIT, i.e., feeling oneself poor, in want, needing help from God, deserving nothing. Remember any examples? (Luke xviii. 13; Romans vii. 24.) Who will feel that most? Those who are trying hardest to be good. They must feel their spiritual poverty, and our Lord says that is a blessed thing. So with you. If you

feel like that, it is much better than to feel proud and self-reliant about your Christian fight.

2. THEY THAT MOURN.—Does it mean mere mourning of any kind for more money, and more fun, and more holidays from school, etc.? No. Though every sorrow brought to Christ will be comforted in some way, yet here we must take it in connection with the "poor in spirit." It means that for the man who feels that need and demerit, it is a blessed thing to think about it and mourn for it. Every true boy or girl who really sees the difference between what he should be and what he is, must surely mourn for it. That is blessed, says the Lord. What is His promise? That is the one sort of mourning of which we may be quite sure "he shall be comforted." But it is possible to hide it from ourselves, and not think or mourn about it. Too busy with lessons, and work, and play, etc. That is a pity. "He who lacks time to mourn lacks time to mend. Eternity mourns that."

3. THE MEEK.—This is the hardest part to teach boys. Boys don't like meekness. They sneer at a meek, chicken-hearted boy, always cowardly and cringing. Does our Lord mean that? Is it wrong to be angry with a sneaking wrong-doer? Is it wrong to thrash a big bully for ill-treating a little chap? Certainly not. That is Christ's will for you, if you can't stop him otherwise. Think of His own awful anger if one injured one of the "little ones" (St. Matthew xxiii. 1, etc.). But then, what about "meek"? It is the feeling that follows on the feelings in (1) and (2). He who knows himself, and how little he deserves, will not be always standing on his dignity, and making the most *of himself*, and flaring

up at every fancied insult *to himself*. Meekness means absence of *self*-assertion. Stand up for weaker ones, and fight for them if necessary, but *not for yourself*. Our Lord dislikes your continually standing up for yourself. Did he ever do it? "Blessed are the meek" means "blessed are they who do not assert themselves and stand up for themselves."

4. HUNGER AND THIRST AFTER RIGHTEOUSNESS.— Same character still. He who feels his want of good, and mourns it, will be the first to hunger and thirst, etc., i.e. to eagerly, earnestly desire to be a noble, righteous boy. What is the promise? Grand promise? I think you all would wish to be good fellows, and please God. But a lazy *wish* won't do. Eager desire—e.g., cycle race, football match—eager, passionate desire to win. As sure as you eagerly desire, says Christ, so surely shall you have it. Pray, "God make me hunger and thirst more, that I may be filled."

5. MERCIFUL.—Same character still. He who has (1), (2), (3), (4), must also be merciful, forgiving, helping the weak, the needy, the unworthy. The world is full of people who will need your forgiveness and kindliness as you go through. The world is full of evil to helpless classes. Child-life in cities, slum people living whole families in one room, poor old people beyond their work, etc.

6. PURE IN HEART.—Means more than common meaning of purity of life. Means "the will set straight towards God." But speak, too, in senior classes, of common meaning. Impurity, above all sins, shuts out

vision of God. See this thought in I*dylls of the King*, where the quest of the Holy Grail was not for Arthur or Lancelot, or even Percivale; only for young Galahad of the white, pure soul.

7. PEACEMAKERS.—Boys and girls often the opposite. Instead of telling your friend the nasty thing some one has said of her, wait till you hear something nice said, and tell her that instead. What is the promise? Will you try to earn it this week? He who is really Christ's servant must always do it. It has a bigger meaning, too, which you will understand better when you grow older. "Not only curers of quarrels," says Mr. Ruskin,[2] "but *peace-creators*—givers of calm, which they must first attain before they can give it." Some of us older people know some of Christ's servants whose very presence seems to make us restful and peaceful in our worries. Sometimes one's mother or dear old friend—a woman oftener than a man.

8. PERSECUTED FOR RIGHTEOUSNESS' SAKE.—Does not seem very blessed, does it? Yet it is wonderful the peace of conscience, the solemn, secret happiness, that Christ gives to the boy or girl willing to suffer for right. It is hard to be jeered at for saying one's prayers or for rebuking filthy talk, etc. Poor coward would not face his comrades' sneers for these. But Christ's brave young soldiers of the Kingdom will do it fearlessly; and Christ is looking, and saying, "Blessed is he who suffers for the Right."

---

[2]*Unto this Last.*

THE SCHOOLING FOR THE KINGDOM

St. Matthew V. 27 to end, and VI. to 25.

§ 1. God's Lower School

Want to talk about God's school for the world, and the various classes, and the lessons to be learned. Did you ever hear teacher in school say, "Now you have learned that lesson. You remember it? Very well; then I am now going to give you a new lesson—a higher and more advanced lesson." Is anything like that in chapter to-day? The Lord Jesus is the great teacher of men from the beginning; and in this chapter, at the founding of His Kingdom, He says: "I am going to give the world a new lesson, higher and more advanced than the last one." Where does He say this? Read ch. v. *vv.* 21, 22, *vv.* 27, 28, *vv.* 31, 32, *vv.* 33, 34, *vv.* 38, 39, *vv.* 43, 44. Which is the old lesson, and which the new? Where are the old lessons found? Old Testament. Who taught them? God Himself, by His appointed teachers. Were they the highest lessons? No; only the elementary lessons for beginners. Now going to give new higher lessons.

Why not give higher lessons long ago? Do teachers in school begin by teaching Latin and Greek and mathematics to the little infant classes? Why not? Is it the incapacity of teacher or pupil? So they begin with the A, B, C, and then lessons a little harder; and so on, and on, and on, waiting patiently for many days, and months, and years, till the gradually growing mind of the child can take in the high teaching. Same in moral and religious training. Slave mission in Central Africa for slaves rescued from the Arabs—poor creatures gathered in from slavery and savagedom, with all their heathen habits strong upon them—with drunkenness, and impurity, and murder, and revenge, quite common, everyday incidents. Missionary cannot begin with higher teaching about loving enemies, and the duty of self-sacrifice, and the perfect consecration of the life to God. Why not? Would not be understood. Begins with lower lessons. God says: "Thou shalt not kill, thou shalt not steal," etc.; and if he can impress on them the sinfulness of these things, he may consider himself for the time fairly successful. By-and-by he hopes to give the higher teaching. And meantime he will often praise them for actions which to us would seem very imperfect. Is he right? Yes, like teacher praising junior class for work which he would think very poor in senior class. By-and-by, when these poor heathens have grown into high-minded Christian men, will they think the old lower teaching wrong as they look back on it? No, they will see it as a lower stage which they have long since passed, but a stage that was a necessary part of their progress upward to the full Christian life.

Why am I talking of these gradual classes in God's school? To help you to understand the Old Testament. Some people are puzzled because the lessons are lower than in New Testament, and because praise is sometimes given for imperfect or faulty acts. A lady came to writer one day, troubled because the Old Testament did not forbid slavery, or putting away a wife, etc. "Why did not God give higher teaching?" she asked. Could you explain to her? Yes; we are in the more advanced classes of God's school now since our Lord came; but the child-races of men in the earlier classes were not capable of our higher lesson, and could only be taught as much as they were capable of receiving. They were often cruel to slaves, often turned away wife out of mere ill-temper. God said, through His inspired teachers: "You must not do that. You must be careful and considerate for the slave, and for the wife who is being put away." They were not yet ready for the higher commands—to set free all slaves; not to put away wives. But they were moving towards it. By-and-by still higher lessons came through the prophets. But they were all like monitors and lower teachers in the school, sent by the Great Master. At last the Great Master Himself came, and now that men had learned the lower lesson, He gave them the new and higher lesson, and the new and higher power to obey it. He founded a High School, with harder and more advanced lessons. Always remember that the coming of Christ made an enormous difference in the world—higher power, higher lessons, higher blessings.

44

§ 2. The Higher School in the Kingdom of God

Now let us take each of the six new lessons. (If not time, teacher should only take one or two.) For example, *vv.* 21, 22. What was the old lesson? Not kill; just as missionary with savage tribe to-day. At the least offence they knock a man's brains out. Missionary does not begin with "Love your enemies"—too high a lesson yet. Enough if at first he can make the man keep from killing—even if he scold, and rage, and get angry; yet, if he keep from killing or striking, it is a good lesson, and a great step gained.

By-and-by teach higher lesson. Next missionary teaches higher still, and so gradually progress is made. What commandment forbids killing? Is it enough for us children of the Kingdom to avoid killing? Have you ever broken the Sixth Commandment? How many people have you killed? If not, how have you broken it? Because you are in the higher classes you belong to the High School—to the Kingdom of God—and therefore more is expected of you. "I am not satisfied," says our Lord, "with your merely not killing people. I go down to the thoughts and intents of the heart. If you hate and revile, and have a murderous feeling, I put you down as breaking my law." So with all the commandments. (In this manner all the six cases given by our Lord can be taught. If there is time, there are many interesting smaller lessons in the chapter, but not room in this Lesson to write about them.)

§ 3. *The Prayer of the Kingdom*

Harder lessons in the new school of the Kingdom; harder work, therefore greater need of help from God. So He teaches His first pupils—His first soldiers of the Kingdom—how to pray. First He teaches how *not* to pray? Yes (*vv.* 1-9). Then teaches them the Prayer of the Kingdom as a *form* of prayer (Luke xi. 2), and an *example* of prayer for ever. Meaning of *v.* 9? Must we only pray *this* prayer? No; may use other prayers, but all in same spirit and manner. It has been said that he who rightly prays the Lord's Prayer must be a high type of Christian. Now, you pray it every day. Do you rightly pray it?

Think of its meaning in future. *Our Father.* Who may use it? May you, even if careless, and having often done wrong? Yes, if you want to. A son may be undutiful, rebellious, prodigal in far country. Yet, if he wants God, he may always cry, "Father" (Luke xv. 17, 18). Must not wait till we feel converted or forgiven, or anything else. So, first feeling is, I am a child, not a slave—though a very unworthy child. I am asking of *our Father;* therefore I may be confident: but *which art in heaven;* therefore I must be reverent and solemn.

Now, how many petitions? First three, then four. Three about God and His will. Four about ____? Which first, God or ourselves? What does this teach? God first, man second. God's glory, and His blessed plans for the world first? my wants and desires last. After this manner always pray. Our first feeling in prayer is, "O God, I want something very badly for myself; please give it to me!" God says, "No, my child, that is not the way to pray. First calm yourself: think of my will and my Kingdom, and all my plans for the blessing of the world. Don't be selfish. Say first, 'Our Father, help all of us together. Never mind me just yet. I want that Thy name may be hallowed, that we may walk before Thee as the great, all-pure, all-holy God. I want Thy Kingdom to come on earth, and Thy will to be done on earth, that life may be the lovely, blessed thing which Thou desirest. Never mind me, Lord, just yet; these are the first things I want.' " Is it easy to pray like that? No, but it will become so, and it will be the greatest blessing to our lives.

Does God let me pray for myself at all? Yes. What are the last four petitions for? Yes, these are our sore wants, and God wishes us to ask about them. But even there He guards against my being selfish. How? Can you see? Say petitions again. Is it "Give *me my* daily bread? Forgive *me my* trespasses," etc.? No, not *me* and *mine*, but always *us* and *our*. I think God must hate selfishness more than anything on earth. He is always watching to stop it even in prayer. Like a father hearing one little chap in his family always asking, "Father, *I* want holidays for *myself*," etc. Father refuses. By-and-by he learns to ask, "*Our* father give us all a holiday—not me alone: I would rather not get it if the others had to work—it would not be fair." Then the father, with glad heart grants the holiday—glad because his boy has learnt the spirit of unselfishness in his requests. Now tell me the two great lessons of the Lord's Prayer.

1. God and His blessed purposes first; I and my wants last.

2. Not *me* and *mine*, but always *us* and *our*.

Now take the petitions in order, and see if it be true that no one can truly pray them unless he is an earnest follower of Christ. *"Hallowed be Thy name."* Meaning? May we think of Thee and walk before Thee as the great, all-pure, all-holy God. Could you pray that truly without trying to be good? *"Thy Kingdom come, Thy will be done."* Where? On earth. How? As it is in heaven. Could you pray that truly without trying to be good? Thy Kingdom come into all hearts—mine and everybody's—that we may be true servants of Thy Kingdom, and make life happy and holy for all. That Thy will may be done. By whom? Me and all others—as it is done in heaven. Think of a boy or girl praying that, and then wilfully doing wrong. What hypocrisy! *"Give us our daily bread,"* i.e., give to me, and to all the poor creatures around me, even to the little robin on the window-sill; give to me and to them by means of me and of all who have power to help. What would you say of a man who prayed that, and then turned away from helping some poor neighbour in want? *"Forgive us,"* etc. What does this force you to do? No unforgiving boy or girl dares use it. It would mean, "Forgive me as I forgive," i.e., "Don't forgive me at all." *"Lead us not,"* etc. Imagine a boy using that prayer, and then tempting another to lie, or do something bad. So on through the whole prayer. Learn to use it thoughtfully, and it will lift up your whole life. Begin to-night. Either the praying will make you leave off sinning, or the sinning will make you leave off praying. You can't do both together, so wonderful is the power of the prayer taught by our Lord.

LESSON V

THE TEACHING OF
THE KINGDOM

St. Matthew VI. 25 to end, and VII.

This Lesson is too long to read. Take the four leading thoughts, and read each of the four sections, or as many as you have time for. Mention the four subjects—(1) Fretting for to-morrow; (2) the beam and the mote; (3) prayer; (4) character the supreme test. I doubt if it be wise to attempt teaching them all in the allotted time.

§ 1. Fretting for To-morrow

Read *vv.* 25-34, noticing the command three times (*vv.* 25, 31, 34), and each time followed by a reason. First, it is needless; second, it is heathenish; third, it is useless and mischievous. This is not a fault of children, and it will need some trouble to interest them in it. Meaning of "take no thought"? Don't fret; don't be anxious. See Revised Version. When our Bible was translated, that was meaning of "taking thought." A book of that time tells of an old city alderman who died of "taking thought," i.e., fretting; and one of the wives of Henry VIII. is said (and I don't wonder) to have been always "taking thought." Does the Lord mean that nobody need be anxious about the future—even careless, wicked people who neglect their duty? He is speaking to his own disciples, who are loving God and trying to do their duty, but are anxious about result; and it is only to such it applies. See *v.* 33: "Seek ye," etc.—i.e., when you are serving God and trying to live your life for Him, you may trust Him to take care of you, and go about as light-hearted as the birds of the air.

Do we not need, then, to plan and work earnestly to prepare for the future? Should we sit still, and leave it to God?—e.g., a boy preparing hard for future business; a father planning and working about children's future. Ought they let it alone, and trust God for it? No, God would be displeased if they did. God has given them brains, and strength, and power to plan, and if they won't use them, they must suffer. God only means, *"When you have done your best* with the powers I gave you, *then* don't fret—trust Me." See illustration—birds of the air live in perfect light-heartedness. But have they not worked and planned? Have you watched nest-building in spring, and all the planning and contriving for the coming young ones? The little birds of the air do everything possible for the future, but with light-hearted happiness, "reposing unconsciously on the purpose of God." Do you know the little sparrow's song?

> "I'm only a little sparrow,
>   A bird of low degree:
> My life is of little value,
>   But the dear Lord cares for me.

51

"I have no barn or storehouse,
 I neither sow nor reap;
God gives me a sparrow's portion,
 But never a seed to keep.

"I know there are many sparrows—
 All over the world they are found—
But our heavenly Father knoweth
 When one of us falls to the ground.

"Though small, we are never forgotten;
 Though weak, we are never afraid;
For the Heavenly Father careth
For the life of the creatures He made.

"I fly through the thickest forest;
 I alight on many a spray;
I have no chart nor compass,
 Yet I never lose my way.

"I just fold my wings at nightfall,
 Wherever I happen to be;
For I know that the Father careth:
 Dost thou know His care for thee?"

This trouble of fretting for the future is not yours yet. You are like the birds. But it is a sore trouble to older people, and may be to you by-and-by. So look at the Lord's three reasons. Find me the first? (*v.* 25); i.e., *It is needless*. You fret about the clothes and food to support life. But He says, "Is not the life itself more important?" And you have to trust God for that. You have to trust Him to settle whether you shall live or die. You may as well trust Him for the lesser things, when you have done your best to provide them. The birds and the lilies, which cannot even do all that we can—cannot reap or sow, or store in barns—yet God takes care of them. Could not you trust Him to care for you?

Second reason (*vv.* 31-33), *It is heathenish.* The heathens have to be anxious, as they don't know of God's care; but you have been taught to think of Him as our Father. Our earthly father cares. Is not God at least as good as he, and as safe to trust?

Third reason, *It is useless and mischievous.* If you fret about to-morrow, to-morrow will still have its own cares when it comes. You don't lighten them by fretting about them to-day. God promises, "As thy day shall thy strength be." Each day gets strength for itself. But if you put forty days' care on to one day, you are not promised strength for that. So people spoil their health, and their tempers, and their work by living in a state of fret, which is a result of not trusting God. Good plan to divide life into days, and "live one day at a time." Each morning pray, "Lord, I want to live a beautiful life *to-day*— to be unselfish, and kind, and pure, and true. I want strength to bear all troubles of *to-day*, and to fight all temptations of *to-day*. I will not trouble about to-morrow till it comes."

§ 2. The Beam and the Mote

Now we come to the Parable of the Beam and the Mote.

Read ch. vii. 1-6. What is condemned here? Does it mean you must not form opinion as to whether a person is good or bad, whether a boy is a sneak or a liar, or whether he is honourable and true? Can't mean that. See *vv.* 17-20, where He tells you to judge by their fruits. What, then, is condemned? The criticising fault-finding temper—seeing motes, looking only for faults and defects, like the carrion-fly on the meat, looking only for the diseased parts. It is God's will that we should distinguish between good and evil. It is God's will that we should condemn evil. What a miserable milk-and-water set we should be if we never rose in fierce, angry condemnation of selfishness, lying, trickery, meanness. Remember how angry He Himself was at all such things. When we read the passage, we see at once that what He condemns is the fault-finders, who are quick and sharp to see failings, but quite blind to beauties and goodness.

What their punishment? (*v.* 2.) Get same treatment from man, and worse still from God. He who is not tender and sorrowful about his comrade's faults cannot belong to Christ's Kingdom, nor receive God's forgiveness. Is this sort of person quick at seeing his own faults? (*v.* 3.) Meaning of seeing mote, and not seeing beam? He is quick to see others' faults, and slow to see his own. Christ wants the very opposite. How does a boy or girl manage to be so blind to own faults? Partly does not like to look for them; partly because we have two different names for a doubtful act—one name when we do it ourselves; the other when some one else does it.

> What I call Rashness in another,
> I call Courage when the act is mine.

What I call Stinginess in another,
   I call Prudence when the act is mine.
What I call Uncharitableness in another,
   I call Keen Judgment when the act is mine.
What I call Revengefulness in another,
   I call High Spirit when the act is mine.

And so on. Thus we manage to make little of own faults, and much of others'. Remember this danger, and watch against it.

Am I not, then, to speak to my comrade, that he may get rid of the fault I see in him? Yes; but what is the first thing to fit me for helping him? (*v.* 5.) Be very keen and sharp-sighted in judging myself, but very gentle in making allowance for another. The member of Christ's Kingdom must be humble, merciful, sympathetic in judging—looking for good rather than evil, putting the kindest construction possible upon others' acts.

Are you to feel bound, then, to believe everything good of every rascal under the sun? No; but you are to judge like Christ, i.e., to judge fairly, to look for the good in them as well as the evil—nay, to look more for the good than the evil, even as He does. That is the great blessedness of dealing with Christ—He is so quick at finding the good: like magnet, so quick in finding the steel in midst of rubbish. Never think of Him as if He were only watching to find and pounce on evil in you. He is always seeking for the least trace of good in you—seeking more earnestly than the poor mother, who tries to find good in her wicked boy. That is, I think, why the Lord Jesus condemns the fault-finder so sharply—he is so opposite to God.

An old legend about His childhood illustrates this. Playing with the Nazareth boys in the evening, they found a little dog dead on the roadside. "What an ugly little beast!" cried they. "How dirty and bloody! What a nasty smell from him!" But when little "Jesus, the carpenter's son," came up, He cried out at once, "What lovely white teeth he has; they are just like ivory!" In the midst of all the ugliness his eye caught the one thing beautiful. Whether the story be true we don't know; but it just describes our Lord, always looking for the good.

Therefore, try to be like Him, looking for the good. There is some good in every boy and girl, and man and woman, in the world, even in the one you most dislike. There is a great deal of good in some of them, if we would get more sharp-eyed to see it, and give them credit for it, instead of being sharp to see the evil, and give them blame for it. Think now of the boy or girl that you think worst of, and see if next week you can't find some good in them or some excuse for them. That will please our Lord.

§ 3. About Praying

Read vii. 7-12. The Lord is here insisting on the need of earnestness in prayer. What are the three directions? (1) Ask; (2) Seek; (3) Knock—i.e. (1) Desire: ask only what you want or care about; (2) Seek it: search for it eagerly, like a gold-digger for the gold; (3) Knock: keep on persistently, importunately. See story of man knocking and keeping on knocking (St. Luke xi. 5, etc.).

Often our prayer so careless—our knock like a boy's "runaway knock"; don't wait for an answer. If we prayed as Christ tells us, we should get far more answers. How does He illustrate God's love? (*v.* 11.) Like a parent, only "how much more" shall your Heavenly Father?

Does this mean that we shall always get whatever we like to ask? Would that be good for us? Would you think a parent good who did that?—e.g. a little child cries for bread-knife at breakfast. Why does he think he should get it? Because he is silly and ignorant, and does not know what is good for him. What does wise parent do? So in *v.* 9 the Lord qualifies promise. "If a child sees a loaf-shaped stone or a coiled-up serpent, and wants it, thinking it to be a loaf or a fish, would father give it?" "No," said the people. Well, He says, God in the same way will keep from you foolish or bad things that you in your foolishness think good. So, in asking for earthly things, first, never act selfishly—e.g., two boys competing for a school prize. Lord, give it to me! That is selfish, and unlike Christ. God does not listen to such. Second, always say: "Lord, only give me what I ask, if it be good for me, and according to Thy will."

But there is one sort of prayer with no limit? Yes; when we ask to be made good, and true, and noble, and lovable. Need not say, "If it be good for me," nor, "If it be Thy will." Why? Yes; we can have as much as we like of God, of goodness, of unselfishness. What a pity, then, not to have more. Fancy going into a bank, and being told you may have as much as you like, and coming away with a few pennies. What grand fellows you boys could be, what high, lovable characters you girls could have, if only you cared more. Just ask, and keep on asking, and seeking, and knocking.

> "It is only God can be had for the asking;
> It is only heaven that is given away."

THE "SIGNS" OF THE KINGDOM

St. Matthew VIII.

§ 1. The Leper

The Sermon on the Mount was over. What impression made? (vii. 28.) And now, like a big congregation after church, the whole crowd come trooping down the hillside on to the Capernaum road, with the Lord in the midst. And all the time a poor skulking creature is watching them, peering at them through the bushes, afraid to come near, yet wanting to come. At last he takes courage, and ventures into the open.

> "A leper, with the ashes on his brow,
>   Sackcloth about his loins, and on his lip
> A covering—stepping painfully and slow,
>   And, with a difficult utterance, like one
> Whose heart is with an iron nerve put down,
>   Crying, 'Unclean! unclean!'"

Poor fellow! what an awful fate! Once young and happy, probably with friends about him, perhaps young wife and children, till the day that the ghastly leprosy appeared in his blood, and he was hunted forth from human society like a dog. No wife, nor child, nor friend for him for evermore. And the fearful crawling disease is spreading—hideous sores, fingers rotting off. And he is half maddened by the isolation, and the loathing and repulsion that meet him everywhere. Sick, and heart-broken, and alone, there is no hope but death.

Perhaps he had hidden and listened to the sermon, and felt his poor, dead heart stirring at the noble kindly words. At any rate, he is going to risk speaking to Christ. Would the crowd like that? No, shrink back, drive him away. It would be defilement if he touched them. But Jesus waited and looked on him. There was no defilement could come to Him. The current flowed the other way. Virtue flowed *out from Him*. Thus it was that He touched our sinful human nature, and healed it without defiling Himself. So He looked sorrowfully at the poor outcast, at the hideous sores, and the rotting, loathsome flesh; and then He did something more loving still. What? TOUCHED HIM! While the people in disgust could hardly look upon the man, Jesus stepped forth, and, like a brother, with a brother's pity and love, laid His hand on the poor fellow. Ah! it was many a long year since human hand in love had touched him; and one can fancy the touch thrilling through his very soul, and binding him to Christ in love for over. And then Christ said:—

> " 'Be clean!'
> And lo! the scales fell from him, and his blood
> Coursed with delicious coolness through his veins;

> And his dry palms grew moist, and on his brow
> The dewy softness of an infant's stole.
> His leprosy was cleansed, and he fell down
> Prostrate at Jesus' feet, and worshipped Him."

Did he ever turn a poor leper or other helpless creature away? Will he ever turn you or me or anyone away if we want His help?

§ 2. *The Officer's Servant*

After leper who next came? Not officer himself, but a little deputation of the chief men of the town (see Luke vii.). He was too humble, had too much reverence for Jesus, to venture himself. Who was this officer? Captain in the Roman army. Had he many chances of being a good man? Foreigner—heathen—doing Roman police work in keeping down sullen people; yet had an "honest and good heart." Even in heathen, ignorant of Christ, there are those differences. True hearts, blindly groping after the light—obeying the dim commands of conscience, and thus, in their poor way, obeying God. And this sort will, *of course*, always be attracted by the teaching of Christ. Why "of course"? Because Christ is the light of the conscience. He lighteth every man coming into the world. (John i. 9.) It is He that is guiding the heathen by means of conscience. Therefore of course, when He more fully appears, the true heart that was trying to obey in the darkness springs forward to Him, and recognises Him at once (see Romans ii. 14, 15).

So you see this man was already attracted by Jewish

Bible and religion. What had he done for them? (Luke vii. 5). Built their beautiful white synagogue, where Jesus sometimes went to church. Show me his kindliness? His humility? There must have been something in our Lord's appearance that had greatly impressed him. He was a soldier, accustomed to recognise a great leader when he saw one, and they had such in the army. Tribunes, consuls, general officers, were sometimes very ordinary men, but sometimes born leaders, and a soldier would feel the difference at once. It is a good thing for boy or man to be accustomed to meet those greater and better than himself, able to guide and lead him; and it is good to learn, when he does meet them, not to envy or backbite or make little of them, but accept and trust them humbly and gladly, and follow them. I think this centurion was thus accustomed to look up to and trust a true man, a true leader; and so, when he knew our Lord, he felt at once that he was in the presence of such. How does he express this? (*v.* 9.) Meaning?

Did the Lord like being thus recognised and trusted? (*v.* 10.) Did He grant his request? As He thinks of this Gentile stranger thus accepting Him by faith, He prophesies of the Gentiles in the far ages to come. What? Who are the Gentiles that have faith to-day? Those who, like that poor heathen officer, recognise Christ, and are touched by the beauty of His life, and yield themselves to Him. Are we such?

§ 3. *"At Even, Ere the Sun Was Set"*

All this time, with the crowd still following, He was

moving on through the town—to whose house?—to dine there probably. Whom did he heal there? That evening a wonderful sight on the strand outside Peter's cottage. Could you describe it? Crowds around the house, sick on mattresses along the shore. Whole strand covered with diseased, and epileptic, and mad people, and those possessed with devils, shouting and yelling— all excitement and disturbance. And in the midst One, undisturbed, unexcited, calming, and quieting, and healing, and blessing. Wherever He came, the calm, and quiet, and blessing came too.

Read hymn, "At even, ere the sun was set," and teach the lessons there suggested. But do not pass over the striking application of prophecy in *v.* 17. He *took* our infirmities, and *bare* our diseases. "Took" means *transferred to Himself—assumed;* and "bare" implies the burden, the oppressiveness to Him. It seems to mean that He performed His miracles of healing, not by some magical or external power, but by Himself bearing in some way the sicknesses which He removed. He wrought His miracles at His own expense. Just as He could only remove sin by bearing the terrible, mysterious burden whose awful, intolerable weight bowed Him down at Gethsemane, so, it seems, He could not remove sickness without in some way losing, suffering, bearing its burden. You remember the case (Mark v. 30; Luke viii. 46) where a woman touched Him from behind, and healing flowed to her. But at a loss to Him, and He instantly turned round as He felt it; and though He saw the crowd touching and crushing, He could distinguish one touch by the outflow of some power from Himself.

"I perceive that virtue hath gone out of me." If we are right that all healing was at His own cost and loss—an outflow of His life—does it not help us to realize how His whole life was one continual self-sacrifice, giving of Himself? And should it not make us reverently adore Him and love Him, and rejoice in the knowledge of the utter self-sacrifice of God?

§ 4. Two Sorts of Disciples

But the crowd was now becoming too oppressive. I suppose to a high-strung nature rejoicing in holy solitude and communion with His Father, this incessant strain and publicity would be unbearable but for His sympathy and love to men. It is getting too trying and disturbing now. "Get me a boat," He says; "we must cross the lake." Soon the report spreads in Capernaum, "He is going to-night." A good deal of excitement.

Story tells of two men who came to speak to Him as He left. Tell me of them. What did each say? What sort of man, do you think, was the first? Impulsive, gushing, with well-meaning, sincere emotion; but too quick and light in resolving—not likely to keep on. Does the Lord refuse him or rebuke him? No, but sobered him to think about his resolve. "Count the cost," He says, "it is not easy work following me." Are there such men to-day? Yes, at missions and times of religious excitement. Like what sort of soil in Parable of Sower?

Now, what sort the next man? His request? Probably does not mean that father was dead, but that he was old, and this young man meant, "I want to stay for the remaining years with my father till I bury him." I don't think our Lord would disapprove of that. But "He knew what was in man," and perhaps knew this one to be of hesitating, vacillating spirit, was always delaying—who wanted to be forced to a decision. So He dealt with each as each needed.

And then he passed on to the boat. Probably, utterly exhausted after all the healing, after all the "virtue gone out" of Him, fell fast asleep. Tell me rest of story. Not time for full teaching. What does it teach? About the Church, that Christ is always in the midst of her, even though at times seeming asleep; and though the storm may howl and danger seem imminent, yet all will come right if she rise and cry to Him. So with ourselves in our individual troubles. He is ever roused by the eager cry of our distress, even if the faith be largely mixed with fear, as in this case.

MORE "SIGNS" OF THE KINGDOM

St. Matthew IX. to v. 35.

Show map of Sea of Galilee. Briefly question on last Lesson. What miracles happened? Where? See Capernaum on map. Why did he leave? Crowds. Where did He go to? How? What happened in crossing? Show Gadarenes' country, and explain why He left (viii. 34). Now we begin to-day's chapter. Back to Capernaum, henceforth called His "own city." Perhaps Virgin Mother had moved there, or He lodged with Peter. At any rate, this was His centre, to which He always returned.

§ 1. The Man Who Came through the Roof

Now read *vv.* 1-9. St. Matthew does not tell this at all as fully as St. Mark or St. Luke. Matthew was probably not there, though he lived in Capernaum. Where was he? He was down at his office at the toll-gate (*v.* 9), and so did not see it. St. Mark gives most interesting picture. (Teacher read Mark ii. 1-5.) Crowds as dense as ever. Stir and excitement all over the place when they found

Him returned. He inside the court-yard with the most intimate friends of the family. Crowds waiting outside to see Him and to be healed. Could not get even near the door.

On outskirts of crowd a poor, paralyzed man carried by four kindly comrades. "Can't we get through?" "No, not a chance. Crowds of sick all round the door. Wait till to-morrow." But these good fellows could not bear the disappointment of their poor friend. Helpless and sick, and with another sore trouble in his heart as well (see below), he longed to get near Jesus, and feared that he should miss Him. What could they do? No hope of getting through. At last a brilliant thought occurred to one of them—the thought that would at once occur to an Irish boy if there. "We cannot get near this house at all. Let us climb up on the roof next door. Then we can climb over the little parapet on to this roof; and then what?" Capital idea! Not the first time that fisherman had used his wits to get out of an awkward place!

Now look inside. Little crowd in the courtyard. *(Place four Bibles on end in hollow square. This is the house, all rooms facing inward towards open courtyard. Now lay a thin book over courtyard as movable roof.)* People in courtyard; Jesus on verandah, seated. Suddenly noise above; light shining in; trap-door removed; tiles stripped off. And in a moment four brown sailor faces, smiling with delight at their clever idea; four cords tied in sailors' knots at corners of the mattress, and down, swinging through the roof, comes the poor frightened paralytic, down to the very feet of the Lord. I can imagine His good-natured smile at the kindly trick. He loved to see people trusting Him, and to see them determined not to be put off. Could He see into these men's hearts? (*v.* 2.) Saw the love and the unselfishness, but, above all, the faith—i.e., the *trust* in Him. He delights in being trusted.

But now see the man on ground looking up with dawning hope. What does he expect to hear Christ say? "Be healed." Does He say it? What does He say? Does not it seem strange to you? Do you think it disappointed the man? Not altogether, I think. Christ read his heart, as well as his friends' hearts. What did He read there? His illness probably result of his own sin; and, I think, in his lonely helplessness and depression he had become sorrowful and penitent. Is this only a guess of mine? How do I know it? Because I know Jesus would not have offered that precious gift of pardon to one careless and impenitent. He read the man's heart. And there is a great lesson here. He gave what He knew to be the greatest gift, the greatest need for man. We think sickness and pain the worst things. God says no—sin is the worst. To be pardoned and made holy is God's highest gift. And this poor man, I think, had begun dimly to see this.

But story not over yet. There were other hearts that He could read? (*v.* 3.) Did they speak out their suspicions? But He knew them. These are the bigoted, uncharitable people who are always looking for faults. They were not touched by the pity on Christ's face, nor the trembling hope of the poor paralytic. The beauty of high character and the sorrows of troubled hearts are not nearly as prominent to this class of men as some fault that they can find out. And so, instead of thinking "He is kind and loving," they only think "He is blaspheming." (Read Mark ii. 7.) But were they not right about power of forgiving sins? Yes, though their feelings were uncharitable. None but God can forgive. Did Jesus then apologize for His words? Not a bit of it. He accepts their challenge at once. True, none else but God has power to forgive. "But I, the Son of Man, have power." Therefore, what follows? Tell me proof He gave them. And the man took up his bed—i.e., mat or mattress. I hope you did not think it a big four-post bedstead! What impression made?

§ 2. St. Matthew's Banquet, and What Came of It

Read over quickly *vv.* 9-18. From *thence*—i.e., from the house—He came out in the evening to walk down by the toll-gate. The collector is in his little office, taking the taxes on the fish, and wood, and cloth, and people passing through. Probably knew Jesus, and was already a disciple, like other apostles. (See Lesson III, §3.) Knew the others had been called to found the new Kingdom; but did not expect that a poor despised "publican" would be. Gladly he rose up and resigned his good situation to follow Christ. Then, next day, he wanted to say good-bye to his comrade publicans. How? Gave a big farewell dinner (Mark ii. 15; Luke v. 29). Not a very fashionable company. People despised and hated these "publicans," and often with good reason, as extortioners and dishonest. But all were not so.

Remember another good publican? (Luke xix. 2.) It was a memorable dinner for them all. First came two disputes. With whom? (*vv.* 11, 14.) Why were Pharisees vexed? What did He answer? Meaning? Yes. "You are such good, superior people in your own eyes, of course, you don't want me. The doctor only comes to those who are sick. You see nothing wrong with you. These poor people feel their sin. I came not to call *saints*, but *sinners.*" So you see it is a very dangerous thing to be insensible to our sinfulness.

John's disciples did not object to publicans. Their own beloved master would not shrink from them. But he was lying now in a dungeon, and they were lovingly, sadly keeping a fast for their sins, as he had taught them. And it hurt them to see Christ's disciples feasting. Our Lord tells them there is a time for fasting for His disciples, but not yet. We can only explain the dispute— no time to discuss question of fasting here.

§ 3. How the Banquet Was Disturbed

For a much more startling interruption came. While he was talking to John's disciples, a noise and commotion at door, hurried footsteps, and a man breaks in on the banquet with his imploring cry to Christ. What? "My little girl is dying—just almost dead; but if you come, it is all right!" How did he know? Why should he think that Christ could heal her? Remember, in last Lesson, the elders of the synagogue sent by centurion (viii. 5; Luke vii. 3-5), who told how their synagogue was built. This man who now rushed in was a ruler of that synagogue—a churchwarden, we might say—and, of course, would have been probably on that deputation, and seen the healing of the centurion's servant. Therefore, he rushed at once to the Lord Jesus in his terror. And Jesus immediately rises from the table and His disciples to go to the ruler's house.

But something happened on the way which made them pause in spite of Jairus' impatience? (*v.* 20.) World very full of trouble. When you try to relieve one case, you find many more. I wonder if Matthew went with them. For here again he does not tell the story as fully as an eye-witness would (see Mark v. 25; Luke viii. 43). Poor woman had been ill since the very year that Jairus' daughter was born. How do you know? Picture the scene carefully, and point out—(1) That Jesus felt the power go out of him, and therefore probably had to perform His miracles of healing at loss and strain to Himself (see last Lesson). (2) That it has a spiritual meaning. Crowd in Church to-day; all seem thronging and pressing about Christ. But do all *touch* Him like this woman, so as to get power and healing from Him? No; only those who, with earnestness and trust, reach out to Him. (3) That Christ accepts very stupid, ignorant faith. She thought superstitiously that the power might be in His clothes. Yet He did not reject her, but taught her to know Him better. Tell story of "Daft Jamie," a poor, half-idiot boy in Scotland, too stupid to be let go to Holy Communion. But he longed to go, and at last the kind minister allowed him. Poor boy was full of joy and excitement all day. "Oh, I hae seen the bonnie Man!" Next morning he was found dead in his bed. In the night-time he had passed away in his joy, and gone to see "the bonnie Man" for ever and ever.

Poor Jairus! Can't you imagine his agony of mind at this delay, and how he would turn away from the woman to watch with feverish eagerness the windows of his house on the hillside? "Oh! my little girl will die before He comes!" And even as he thinks of it, he hears galloping hoofs, and sees his servant approach. One glance at the man's face is enough. "Too late! Your little daughter is dead. No use troubling the Rabbi now!" Poor Jairus! But Jesus's ear was quick to hear that message, and his eye meets the poor father's glance. "Don't be frightened; only trust me still!" Hard to trust now. Christ had healed sickness, but never raised the dead before. Half-frightened, half-hoping, the poor father went on. Picture hired mourners, such as exist still in country parts of Ireland. Jesus's curt, stern command to them. Then, with father, and mother, and three disciples (which?), He goes into the little girl's shaded room, where she lay, all silent and still, in her little bed, with the curtains drawn tight around it. What was the matter? Dead? What did he call it? Why? Because, since His coming, death is softened into sleep for all who love Him. They shall waken when He comes back. So Christians try to put away ugly old name (John xi. 11; 1 Thessalonians iv. 14), and put the word "sleep" on their tombs, instead of "death." "She only sleeps," said the Lord, and went to awake her. How? By strenuous, repeated effort, like Elisha? (2 Kings iv. 34.) By praying, like Peter, that God would raise her? (Acts ix. 40, 41.) No. In calm, quiet power, just touched her hand and wakened her—perhaps in the very words by which her mother wakened her every morning, "Wake up, my little girl." "My little girl." He was so fond of these pet expressions of affection. Twice already in this chapter? (*vv.* 2, 22.) "Cheer up, my son—my daughter." And now, "My little girl." The words must have stuck in Peter's memory always; and long years afterwards, when telling the story to St. Mark, he remembered the very word *Talitha*, the diminutive of endearment in the popular language used by the Lord. *Talitha cumi* (Mark v. 41). What is the lesson of the whole story? The kindly sympathy of the Lord in trouble, and the great power of faith or trust in Him.

HOW THE KING SENT FORTH AMBASSADORS

St. Matthew IX. to end, and X.

Divide this Lesson into sections. (1) (ix. 35 to end). Why He sent out the twelve. (2) (x. 1-6). The Twelve. (3) (*vv.* 6-15). The Credentials and Proclamation, and their means of support. (4) (*vv.* 16-33). God's care for them in dangers and persecutions. (5) (*vv.* 34-39). Disturbances wrought by religion. (6) (*v.* 39 to end). Reward for receiving Him and His. Indicate the sections and subjects beforehand.

§ 1. Why He Sent Them (ix. 35 to end)

What is the title of this Lesson?

What are ambassadors?

We have learned about King founding the Kingdom, teaching its laws, doing its deeds; but all the time *by Himself,* unassisted by others. Did He intend to go on always thus? How do you know? (See ch. v. 1; compare Mark iii. 13, 14; Luke vi. 13-20.) Before Sermon on

Mount He had already chosen twelve out of His disciples—for what purpose? Not yet sent them out, but was training them. How? (Mark iii. 14.) Keeping them *with Him*. Was it not a grand training for helpers? If you and I are to be His helpers, same training needed. How? Much with Him in prayer, and thought, and study of His life. They were every day seeing His love, His unselfishness, His helpful deeds, His deep communion with God all through the lonely night. So they were learning His aims, and the meaning of His Kingdom.

But now the time is come for them to go to their work. Why? (*v.* 36.) Crowds increasing, want, misery, sickness, ignorance. His heart is sore and strained with their pain. His sympathy very deep. Man of sorrows, but not His own sorrows. Sorrow of the people. We, in our selfish thoughtlessness, have little idea how terribly that must have pressed on the tender heart of Christ. It is told of a great Englishman—Denison Maurice—that he was one day admiring Da Vinci's beautiful fresco of the Last Supper; and as he looked on the face of St. John, sweet, and gentle, and unlined by care, "What!" cried he, "that the face of the Apostle of Love! How should his face be smooth and unlined? Surely in this world of wrong and misery he must have had more furrows in his cheeks than all the other Apostles?" "And," says Kingsley—who tells the story—"as I looked upon the furrows of his own face, I knew that he spoke the truth—of St. John and of himself likewise—and I understood better from that moment what was meant by Jesus Christ's bearing men's sorrows and carrying their infirmities."

As you think of our Lord on earth, always think of

75

Him with the sorrows and sins of the people pressing on His heart. I suppose that is the reason of the tone of sadness that runs through His life. Always pain for the sake of others. What do they look like to Him? Sheep distressed and scattered (R.V.), having no shepherd to care for them. Remember other times, when He thought of them as sheep wanting Him as shepherd? (St. Mark vi. 34.) Without Him and His beautiful Kingdom of Heaven this would be an awfully miserable, helpless world. Sheep without shepherd. Even now it is so, though you are too young to see it all. Boys and girls without Christ—cross, and peevish, and selfish, and self-indulgent, and therefore not happy. Big men and women without Him too. Could they have Him if they liked? But some poor creatures have hardly a chance at all. Who? Poor, dark heathen in their ignorance and abominable lives, so sorely needing to be lifted up by His Gospel. Men, women and children at home, living in horrible slums, whole family crowded together to sleep, eat, talk, play, wash, cook dinner, etc., all in one filthy, ill-smelling room. Often drunkenness, and swearing, and wickedness of every kind about them. A friend of writer's met little boy in Dublin slum lately. "What time do you go to bed, Tommy?" "Not till very late, sir." "Why not?" "Because I sleep with father, and he is never quiet or good-tempered till he is quite drunk. So I have to wait till then every night." They are born in this vileness, and cannot escape. Almost impossible to grow up good. And the poor people have not the heart or the strength to struggle up out of it. What would our Lord say of them, and of the heathen? Would he despair of them? Would He be disgusted with them? No. He would be full of compassion, and call His servants to pity them, work for them, pray for them. Was this first time of pitying them? Had been always pitying them from heaven. It was pity brought Him down.

§ 2. A Talk about the Twelve (x. 6-15)

So He had to appoint assistants—could not look after all Himself. Besides, would soon be going back to heaven, and wanted to leave His new "Kingdom of God" properly officered for the future. How many were His chief assistants? They were the first officers of the Church, the first bishops. Before dying they appointed other bishops, and these appointed others again, and so down through all the ages to the bishops of the Church to-day, coming down in unbroken succession from the Lord and His Apostles.

Tell me names of the twelve. Notice that they are in six pairs. Why? (See Mark vi. 7.) "Sent them *two and two*." I think that is the reason. These are the six pairs of comrades. The Lord wanted them to help and cheer each other, so did not send alone. Any brothers? Good to have brothers helping each other in doing God's work. Any rich or great? Why not? I suppose because none such had joined Him yet. If Paul or Nicodemus or other such had joined, their education would probably be an advantage to the work. Yet I think it was not a bad thing that all were but simple, common men. Why? Shows completely how Divine is Christianity. Think of a few common, ignorant fishermen turning the world upside down, and changing the whole course of history. Did they? No. God did, and used poor, humble men to do it. If He had used very clever men, people might have thought all was due to their cleverness.

See, too, what different sorts of men. Peter, impulsive and blundering; Thomas, cautious and doubting; Matthew, a despised tax-gatherer; Simon the Zealot, like an Irish Nationalist, a fierce agitator against the Government; and so on. All different in appearance, in temperament, in ability, in character. All alike in what? Loving Christ and hungering after righteousness. In Christ's service there is a place and a work for all sorts of men and women, all sorts of boys and girls. And He has the power of attracting all sorts, if they only come near and know Him. But until they love Him and hunger after His righteousness they are of no use to Him as workers.

§ 3. Ambassadors—Their Credentials, Proclamation (x. 6-33)

You know what ambassadors go to do? Deliver king's message or proclamation? How do people know they are from the king? They bring credentials, perhaps a letter or king's ring, or something to show. What did these bring? (v. 8.) Power to do kind, helpful things. Deeds of love, and mercy and kindness are very good signs that one is sent by God. What was their proclamation? (x. 7.) What did this mean? A something up in heaven or down on earth? (See Lesson III.) Are there any ambassadors of the Kingdom now? Clergy all sent as

Christ's ambassadors (2 Corinthians *v.* 20). Grandest office in the whole world, and the most blessed if in earnest about it. Do you boys ever think of this office in planning your future? We want ambassadors at home in the parishes. We want especially men to go out to the heathen abroad. Think about it. Perhaps God will give some of you this high privilege.

How should these twelve be supported? Take plenty of food, and money, and everything? No (*vv.* 11-15). Why not? Must learn dependence on Him. Ambassadors for King. He will be responsible for them. Must learn to trust Him, and He will put it into people's hearts to feed and lodge them as they go on. Best for them to feel dependence.

But what about the dangers, persecutions, ill-treatment, etc.? Would He not let such things happen? Were they to shirk danger? (*v.* 33.) Were they to court danger? (*v.* 23.) God's rule for them is rule for every Christian—"Trust in God, and do the right." Only ask, What is right thing to do? Never ask, What will happen if I do it? Leave that to God. But will He let the painful consequence fall on me? Yes, if it be best for you. Trust Him for that. But how do I know whether He will notice it? I am very insignificant. What is Christ's answer? (*vv.* 29-31.) "Two sparrows for a farthing"—not much value, surely. So little value, that if you bought two farthings' worth, you would get one thrown in (St. Luke xii. 6.). Yet, as you hear them twittering on the housetops, remember Christ says that God is caring for them. He sees if a stone is thrown at them. Therefore, much more will He care for us, "of more value than many sparrows."

So we are to go forward boldly confessing Him before men. Meaning of confessing Him? Saying Creed? Saying, "I believe He is God"? Not only that, but the habitual acknowledgment by word and deed, all your life long, that He is your Master, and that nothing on earth shall turn you aside—no mockery, no sneers, no careless living of those about you. Baptismal vow puts it exactly right for you, "to be Christ's faithful soldier and servant unto life's end." Then you can always be glad, for Christ is keeping you and watching over you.

§ 4. Closing Words

Strange words in *vv.* 34-39. The sword sent. Surely Christ came to send peace. Yes, but in an evil world there must often be war in order to win peace. He purposes to change the world into the likeness of heaven. But there are many who don't want this, and fight against it, and try to hold us back. Are we to yield to them for the sake of peace? No, says our Lord, not even to father and mother. Nothing on earth must stand higher than right, i.e., higher than Christ. If you love even father and mother more than you love Christ's will, i.e., if you would do what is wrong, and be disloyal to Him, even for their sake, you are not worthy to be His disciple.

LESSON IX

DISCOURAGEMENTS

St. Matthew XI.

§ 1. The Black Castle of Machaerus

John the Baptist was in prison. Remember when we heard of him last? (Lesson II.) What has happened meantime, that he should be in prison? (Mark vi. 17, 18.) He had dared to rebuke the king for his wickedness. It takes a fearless and righteous teacher to act like that, and kings are not very much accustomed to such treatment.

The queen was greatly vexed, and she made Herod seize the Baptist, and shut him up in the Black Castle at Machaerus, on the dreary, desolate shores of the Dead Sea. If any place could break down the spirit of John—accustomed to the free, wild life of the desert— it was that prison. The ruined dungeons are existing still, with the holes in the masonry for the iron bars, to which probably John was chained. There he had lain for about a year when our story opens, with the chains, and bars, and the foul air of the dungeon around him, and outside nothing to be seen through the gratings but the black, bare rocks, and the dreary, desolate sea. No wonder fits of doubt and depression should come on him at times.

During this time he would, of course, be eagerly listening for news of Christ, wondering if Christ were doing all that he had prophesied of Him. What? (Matthew iii. 12.) I think John was puzzled by the gentleness of the Lord. Where is the axe at the root of the trees, and the strong winnowing-fan that should sweep the chaff into unquenchable fire? John was of the sterner, harder type—the fighters and wrestlers, like Elijah, like John Knox, like the many fighters for God who had not time for gentler thoughts. So he is puzzled about the gentle attitude of Jesus. He does not see that the time for the axe and the fan is only to come when all the gentle, loving means have failed.

Who told him about Jesus? (Luke vii. 18.) Evidently his disciples were allowed to visit him. They told of kindly miracles, but of other things too. They were jealous for their own dear master fretting out his heart in prison, while all men were running after the new Teacher (John iii. 26). So, I dare say, they would talk of the prejudices against Jesus, about His breaking the Sabbath rules, and eating and drinking with publicans and sinners. And altogether poor John, in his depression and misery, got puzzled and doubtful even about the Lord. "Could I be mistaken? Perhaps He is not the 'Coming One,' but only another messenger like myself. At any rate, I know He is from God, and He will tell me truth. I'll send two disciples."

§ 2. The Answer to John

So the two disciples started. It took about three days to get from Machaerus to near Nain, where Jesus had just raised the widow's son. When John's disciples arrived, what was He doing? (Luke vii. 21.) So they stood in the crowd, and watched the healing of diseases and plagues, the casting out devils, and restoring the blind. After this it must have seemed to them silly to ask their question. But they do: "John the Baptist hath sent us. Art Thou the 'Coming One,' or look we for another?" What did Jesus reply?

In saying this, He is really almost quoting the very words of two great prophecies which He and John had learned long ago (Isaiah xxxv. 5, 6; lxi. 1). He knew John would understand, and He wanted to comfort him. But He adds a little word of rebuke, too, at the end (*v*. 6). You see, it was very unpleasant, this publicly expressed doubt. His disciples did not yet believe very strongly on Him. He could not trust their faith. And now the strong, brave John, who had borne public witness to Him, begins to doubt. I think it would hurt and disappoint the Lord, and I think it would be likely to have a bad effect on the multitudes.

But was He angry with John? How do you know? (*vv*. 7, 8.) I think it is beautiful to see the kindly carefulness to defend John's character to the crowd, who would be inclined to think less of him on account of his doubting message, sent in an hour of weakness and despondency.

And there is something else very beautiful. Did

He praise John to his disciples' face? No; He even gave them a little word of rebuke to take back. But the moment their backs were turned He bursts out into the most enthusiastic praise of the poor prisoner. I hope somebody told John about this before he died. For a very little while after, you know, Herod sent and cut off his head; and I think it would be a great comfort if he knew what the Lord had said. Do you think he knows it now in Paradise? What is the lesson for us from Christ's dealing with John? The world praises a man to his face, and speaks sharply of him behind his back. The Lord does the very opposite, and He means you to do the very opposite. If your friend has a fault, don't be afraid to tell him to his face, because you love him and want him to be better. But never talk of his faults behind his back, nor let others talk of them to you; and always be more willing to give praise than blame.

What high position does He claim for John? (*v.* 11.) Why? (*v.* 10.) Because he was the herald of the King. True, He praises John for his own sake, just before for his firmness and courage. But all that would not make him "more than a prophet." So remember, in the sight of Heaven the highest honour comes through connection with Christ, being His servant, doing His work. Yet there is a curious thing about the little one in the Kingdom being greater. Wonderful what high value the Lord Jesus sets on this Kingdom of His, into which you and I have been brought! Such an enormous difference has been made in the world by the coming of the Kingdom and the King, that the greatest of the wise and holy men of the old world are inferior even to little ones in the Kingdom, inferior in position and privilege to you if you are Christ's true child. Not only new teaching, but new power, new life, has come into the world with Christ. It is easier for us to know about God, and easier to fight our sins, and to live high, noble, unselfish lives.

What is meaning of "This is Elijah"? (*v.* 14.) (See Malachi iv. 5.) God had prophesied that another Elijah should come. You remember about Elijah, stern, grim, and solitary, with his solemn message of repentance, and of God's wrath against sin. How he rebuked King Ahab for his evil deeds, as John rebuked Herod. They were of the very same type—stern, and fiery, and eager for right, and fearing nothing in the world, except to grieve God. So John was a second Elijah.

§ 3. Judgment on Those Who Rejected the Lord

Probably some of the crowd were pleased that He should praise John, for John was greatly honoured as a prophet. But there were others who were against John and against Jesus alike. There was no pleasing them. They blamed John for fasting, and they blamed Jesus for eating with people, and mixing in their society.

He remembers some old game of "weddings and funerals" that the Nazareth children used to play when He was a little boy. "You are like a set of sulky children, that won't play at any game; while the others call to you and say, 'We played "weddings," and you would not join; we played "funerals," and you still kept away.' We cannot please you!" What was really wrong with these people? They did not want to be good. They did not care seriously about religion. They only cared to find fault with all who were trying to help them towards God.

Now look at the next verses (20-24). See what a great, high claim He makes for Himself. He speaks as judge of all the world, and tells these towns what would happen to them in the Judgment. He knew, for He was Himself the Judge who should pronounce the doom.

Why was the woe pronounced on Chorazin and Bethsaida? (*v.* 20.) Just think of it. "Most of his mighty works," and we scarcely hear a word about them in the Gospels! Does not it show what an immense number of miracles must have been that we hear nothing about? Why was Capernaum condemned? Why, it was "His own city." Most of His time spent there. The people had every opportunity of being attracted by His life, and convinced by His miracles. But, after waiting and hoping all this time, He has to condemn them at last (*v.* 24). Think of Sodom and Gomorrah still waiting for judgment. All the past world, remember, is waiting still. The final Judgment is to be—when? When He "shall come again to judge the quick and the dead." Why "more tolerable for Sodom"? etc. Men are judged fairly, according to their light. Sodom was fearfully wicked; "but," says our Lord, "if they had your chance, it would have been different." And so there is absolute fairness in God's judgment. Every little thought, and act, and deed is taken into account; every hindrance that a man could not help will be noticed by God, to make the punishment lighter. Don't forget that we are in the full light, with every chance of knowing our Lord, and living for Him. It shall certainly be more tolerable for Sodom than for us if we are neglecting the high, unselfish life which God desires for us.

§ 4. *His Comfort in Those Who Accepted Him*

Had He any comfort to balance all these discouragements? (*v.* 25.) As He thought of all who would not receive Him, there comes as a relief the thought of the simple, childlike hearts who did receive Him. "Those scribes and Pharisees, and people who think themselves so wise and prudent, have rejected Me in their conceit. Their conceit has hid the truth from them. God's law is, that conceit, and selfishness, and such things, shall hide truth from men. But I thank Thee, O Father, for the babes, the simple child-hearts of men and women, who feel their need of Me, and want to follow Me." Think how the Lord is pleased and comforted by each one of us who accepts Him as leader. You and I can give Him that comfort.

Now tell me His grand invitation to all who labour and are heavy-laden? Some people are labouring, and find it hard to be good in spite of their efforts; some are heavy-laden with sorrow and pain. What does He promise them all? Rest, peace. You are too young to fully understand this need. But when you grow up, you will see how the world is full of restless, unpeaceful faces, and who, if they would but turn to Him and give themselves up to His guidance, would have rest and peace. He does not always take away the temptation nor the sorrow. But He gives men power to conquer the temptation, and He gives high, beautiful, unselfish aims, that make life noble and true; and He gives comfort and hope to the sorrowful and troubled. You know He used to be a carpenter, and make "yokes" for drawing loads. And if the yoke fitted easily, and was well made, it would enable the animal to draw the load better. I wonder if He had that idea in His mind. "You have the load of temptation and trouble to draw. You are trying to drag it on by clumsy brute force. Take My yoke on you. It will make the load fit more comfortably—it will make it more easy to draw." Temptation and trouble have to be met with in any case. The Lord does not promise to remove them from us. It would not be good for us. But with His "yoke" upon our shoulders, and His Divine strength and comfort in our hearts, they will be easier to bear. Nay, they will be transformed into blessings.

HOW TO KEEP SUNDAY

St. Matthew XII. to v. 38.

The chief lesson to be learned to-day is the way to think of our Sundays. Although the Jewish Sabbath does not quite correspond to the Christian Sunday, yet our Lord's teaching about the right spirit of keeping the Sabbath expresses exactly the way in which we should think of Sunday.

§ 1. Going to Church through the Fields

The Lord Jesus was very careful about attending the public worship of the Church. Even though the clergy were often bad, and careless, and hypocritical, yet the Church was the Church, and no fault in the individual minister could excuse any man for neglecting his opportunities of the regular worship of God. Remember this when you grow up. You may move to a parish where, for some reason, you may not be attracted by the clergyman. That sometimes may happen through the fault of the clergyman. It very much oftener happens through people unreasonably taking up prejudices, and not trying to think the best and make the best of him. It is so easy to be sharp and censorious towards one's pastor, easy to misunderstand a man, and put unfair constructions on some word, or act, or manner.

But the important lesson here is that the Jewish clergy, and scribes, and teachers as a body were *really* bad, cruel, and hypocritical, and hostile to Christ; and yet He and His disciples went regularly to church to be ministered to by these men. Even after the chief priests had crucified Him, still the Apostles went regularly to the Temple worship, and kept the regular hours of prayer. We hear of them at worship at the third hour, the sixth hour, the ninth hour. They had their Temple prayer-book and their Synagogue prayer-book, with fixed services of prayers, and psalms, and lessons from the Scripture, rather like our own; and no fault in the minister could spoil those for them. No fault in any clergyman can spoil the beautiful Liturgy of the Church for you. Therefore, there is no excuse either for staying away from church or for wandering to places of worship that are set up outside the Church. This latter sentence is not unkindly meant towards any religious body. "Grace be with all those who love the Lord Jesus Christ in sincerity." But many good, loving people do not see the evil they do by splitting up the number of the baptized Christians into separate little sects, against the will of Christ. And Church children must not think lightly of this evil.

Going to church, did they go by the road or through the fields? What happened on the way? Just think of the poverty of Jesus when His disciples were so hungry going through the fields. Was He Himself hungry? Be sure He did not eat food if there was not enough for them. Besides, by comparing His case with that of David (*v.* 3), He seems to suggest that "He was hungered, as well as they that were with Him." Did you ever pluck ripe wheat-ears, and rub them on your hands? Did it seem like work, like Sabbath-breaking? Yet some silly people in our Lord's day thought so. Straight behind the disciples were the spiteful Pharisees from Jerusalem, spying on them. They were glad to see them break one of their wretched little Sabbath rules, which said that to pluck an ear of corn was to reap, to rub it was to thresh; and so, they said, the disciples were reaping and threshing on the Sabbath Day! What a silly, stupid thing to say. Had God given an order against reaping and threshing on the Sabbath? Why? In order that the poor, tired workers should be happy and restful, and that no cruel master should work them on the day of rest. It was a kindly, loving order of God. Was it kindly and loving when enforced by these Pharisees? What should they have rather done? Pitied the men for being hungry, and asked them to come and eat with them. Ah! that was not their way of showing religion. That was Christ's way. They would much rather try to find fault, and pretend it was for the sake of religion.

What two examples does Jesus quote? First means that any mere *ceremonial* law about worship must give place to urgent bodily necessity. The great law of Right and Wrong must not be broken for any necessity. It is better to die than to do wrong. But a mere rule about worship is on a different level. But what means second

91

example? What has it to do with the case? (See *vv*. 6-8.) "I am God, where I stand is a Temple—is holy ground. These poor followers of mine, acting in my service, are as guiltless as the priests in the Temple on the Sabbath. And if ye were kind and merciful men, ye would not have condemned the guiltless."

§ 2. In Church

So they went on to church. And the Pharisees went too, and sat in their places at the top, and watched with scowling faces as Jesus entered with His disciples. What had these Pharisees gone to church for? To pray to be made loving, and kind, and good? Not a bit of it. (See Mark iii. 2.) To watch Him. What wicked, spiteful men! Did not like Christ, because He was so real and true; He hated cant and hypocrisy, and sternly rebuked them for it, even before the people. So they lay in wait, and set traps for Him. I suspect this whole affair in the Synagogue was a trap laid by them; that they had put that man there to induce Jesus to break their rules, and then watched to try if they could catch Him. Reading the accounts in the different Gospels leaves that impression.

What ailed man? (*v.* 10.) One of the old lost Gospels says he was a stone-mason, and had told the Lord that he could not earn bread for his family. Picture—village church—man on seat—arm hanging dead—his eager eyes fixed on Jesus. Jesus' pitying eyes on him. Now see the Pharisees whispering and watching. Oh, this wicked Sabbath-breaker! going to heal a man on Sabbath! Hear them call out to stop Him. "Is it lawful to heal," etc. (*v.* 10). His reply (Mark iii. 4). Is it better on Sabbath to do *good*, as I am doing, or to do *harm* by neglecting to relieve misery? Then He appeals to their compassion. How? (*v.* 11.) Yes. "You surely would pull out the sheep. Would you do less for a poor human being? Wherefore it is lawful to do good on the Sabbath Day." All this time the poor man waiting with his dead arm by his side. What next? Could he stretch it forth? Was it not dead? Yes; but when Christ told him, the poor fellow tried to do it, and *with the effort to obey came the power.* So with us—weak, powerless—can't love God, can't conquer sin, can't be truly faithful. But let us say, "Lord, I can't love Thee much; I can't serve Thee as I should; I can't be good as I ought; but, Lord, I'll try!" and *with the effort to obey will come the power.*

Do you think the poor stone-mason was glad? And the people? And the Lord? Were the Pharisees? What did they do? Went out to make plans against Him, and so went on and on in this wicked spitefulness, till they brought the Lord at last to the Cross on Calvary.

§ 3. How To Think of Sunday

Was it right for the Pharisees to be careful about keeping Sabbath? Yes; but they were so silly about it, and so spiteful, they forgot God's loving purpose for it. They would make Sabbath a torment. Did God give Sabbath to be a torment to people? What does the Lord tell the Pharisees about it? (Mark ii. 27.) *Made for man,* i.e., for man's blessing and happiness. Does God like to see happy faces on Sunday? Like to see us out in fresh air, enjoying this beautiful world? Yes, we are His children, and He made Sunday for our happiness, and recreation, and rest. No Latin, or sums, or hard school-lessons to-day for boys and girls. No work for tired men and women. What an awful world if no Sundays! God says to us every Saturday night, "Come ye apart and rest awhile. I want you to rest and be happy." "This is the day that the Lord hath made: let us rejoice and be glad in it." Is it not good of our Father in Heaven? What a shame to make it gloomy!

But something else needed besides rest? We have another part of us besides bodies? Souls. And God, who wants us to be happy, knows that a good, noble, beautiful life will best make us so. He says, "If My children only think of rest and amusement, they may forget about goodness and about My love for them, and so lose their highest happiness. The busy men and women may forget Me in the hurry of their work; so I want to remind them about Me every Sunday, and keep them near to Me." Emphasize the two sides. (1) The rest and recreation for the body. (2) Helps and reminders for the soul. And all *for the purpose of our good*, to make us happy, and holy, and loving to God and man.

Now, the Pharisees forgot the happy meaning of Sabbath. Thought of as of a taskmaster's order to his slaves: "Don't do this, don't do that on Sabbath, or else I will punish you." Our Lord was vexed at the way they were spoiling God's beautiful gift, and so He often, in order to teach them, intentionally broke through their silly rules, intentionally worked miracles on

Sabbath—broke the Sabbath, they would say. It is a great loss and pity when boys and girls are taught to think of Sunday as the Pharisees did. As if God's purpose were to worry and restrict you, and forbid all the things you like, and make you feel that it is only unpleasant things that are religious. I am so afraid of you, children, taking up the silly notion that Sunday is an irksome thing, and that it would be nicer for everyone to be free to do what he liked.

§ 4. Danger of Losing Sunday

If you examine the different passages in the Bible, even about the old Jewish Sabbath, you will find that the two chief directions about it were:

1. "Thou shalt rest from thy work on this day."

2. "Thou shalt *rejoice* and *be glad* in it."

True, they were not allowed to do as they pleased about it. Many would prefer working and making their servants work; many cried, When will the Sabbath be gone? that they might buy and sell, and get gain (Amos viii. 5, etc.), and wring the last drops of sweat out of those who served them. But God allowed no evasion—"Thou shalt do no manner of work, . . . nor thy manservant, nor thy maidservant, nor thy cattle," etc. Can't you see what a kindly rule it was—how many a poor Jewish labourer, with weary limbs and aching head, learned to thank God, and rejoice in His rest, that no greedy, tyrannous master could deprive him of.

And can't you see what a great and blessed thing it is

still, even for this lower advantage of bodily rest—how, in the terrible strain and competition of these days, we ought to thank God for His law of Sunday. What fools people are when they talk of Sunday as a restriction placed on them. I wonder how you children would like doing your school-work just the same Sunday and week-day. Well, men and women will come to have to do their work every day alike if Sunday is lost to them. They ought to guard it rather as a precious heritage. I see great danger of losing it altogether in these days. It is a good thing to get people out into the country, and let them enjoy nature. But I see more and more, under the excuse of this, how men are being deprived of their Sunday rest. I see shops getting to be opened more than they used. I know men that do not get one Sunday off work in a year. I see tram-drivers and railway-men moving into slavery where seven days' work will be exacted for six days' pay. And, in the fear of all this, we want you young people to see God's good purpose in the Day of Rest, and fight hard that your country should not lose it.

I need not remind you that there is even a more important thing than bodily rest—that our lives should be made noble, and peaceful, and true, and good. For this we must have religion. For religion we must have our Sundays.

Remember, then, that the Sabbath was made for man—for man's body, his soul, his happiness, his peace—and never think of Sunday except as a great blessing from God.

SEVEN PICTURES OF THE KINGDOM

St. Matthew XIII. 18 to end.

Remind what a parable is, and why Christ taught by parables. Then point out that it is impossible to teach seven parables in detail in one Lesson; therefore can only glance briefly at them, and try to see their connection and meaning. Better be content with a rough notion, without going into nice refinements of the meaning. For this purpose point out that in the Lesson there is—first, The Parable of the Sower, and then three *pairs of parables:* (1) The Mustard-seed and the Leaven; (2) The Hid Treasure and the Pearl of Great Price; (3) The Tares and the Draw-net. Let them find these before reading the chapter. Better stop at *v.* 50, unless there is plenty of time.

§ 1. *The Picture of the Four Sorts of Hearers*

Which would be more interesting to children—a long, prosy sermon, or a set of short stories and pictures? I think our Lord must have been a very interesting speaker to simple people or children. The people used to crowd about Him, and He always taught them— by what? Long, tiresome sermons? No (*v.* 34). The disciples could understand more serious and difficult discourses; but he always spoke to the simple people in little parables and word-pictures. As He spoke His little word-pictures, the people used to make the picture, each for himself in his mind. In this chapter we have one long word-picture of the Sower, and then *three pairs* of shorter word-pictures; and all were to teach lessons about the Kingdom of God.

Now, I tell the word-pictures, and you shut your eyes, and make the picture in your mind as I go on, just as the Lord and the people did as He sat by the lake.

First picture rapidly the Sower. The teacher should know this Lesson well enough. It is taught fully in this series of Sunday School Lessons (Lessons on St. Mark). At any rate, there is not room to give it fully here. Point out at the close that it would be in some degree discouraging to the disciples—only one part in four of the good seed bringing forth fruit. But there are other lessons in other pictures. Now we take them in pairs, make the picture first, and then read the parable.

§ 2. The Pictures of the Little Germ Becoming the Great Kingdom

Now for a pair of little pictures together. But first see in my hand all these little specks. Some are seeds; some are little specks of glass, or wood, or other dead things. What difference between the seeds and the others? Which the greatest? What would happen if I put them all into the earth of the garden?

I see in my mind a man and a woman. The man is putting in the ground the seed of a tree. The woman has a pan of flour near the fire, and she is putting into it a little liquid substance called leaven. They go away. All is just as it was—unchanged. But I come again and look. I see the little seed become a great tree, shelling the buds. I see the pan of dough rising and moving, and overflowing the vessel. Now, this little pair of pictures is to encourage the people discouraged by the story of the Sower. Why discouraged? How encouraged now?

Don't you see? This Kingdom of God as yet was such a tiny thing—only a few ignorant disciples, led by a poor Galilean carpenter. How could it do anything? Yet Christ had taken these men from their work, and sent them out to found a great kingdom which should cover the world. How silly and hopeless it looked! What chance of success could it have?

But the Lord bids them think of the little seed, so tiny and useless-looking—scarce distinguishable from a bit of dead matter. But *because it has life* it is bound to become a tree. Look at little acorn. What if I put it under the earth? It *must grow* into a great oak, because it has a mysterious power implanted in it by God. Could you keep it down? Not even if you put two big stones on the top of it? No; it would grow between them, and force them back by that tremendous mysterious power in it, and, in spite of them, would go on to fulfil its purpose, and become a great oak. Yet, when I put it underground, does it seem at first to make any difference? Do I get uneasy because it is lost and hidden, and I cannot see it? No; because it is a living seed, it is bound to come up.

What seed did the Lord sow? His life and death of self-sacrifice for men. When men learned that God had done that for them, it would touch their hearts, and spring up into a beautiful life for Him. So the Lord was not a bit uneasy about His small numbers, and His short life and humiliating death. "They are the seed," He said, "and will grow, and grow, and grow for ever."

Is His prophecy coming true? Yes, growing and growing. Now, after 1900 years, it shows no sign of stopping its growth. The greatest days are all before it. The whole Church that day could fit in this class-room. Where could it fit now? And with the new century there is rising a great hope, a great enthusiasm, in the Church. Probably this twentieth century will be the grandest century of its growth; and so the centuries will go on.

But how does it grow? Like the leaven (explain leaven), dropped into the dead dough, makes it stir and grow. So the leaven of Christ's Gospel gets into us, and makes us stir and grow; and we become leavened, and leaven others. All is by influence. Therefore, the best thing any boy or girl can do for Christ's Kingdom is—what? To be good—to be true, loving, Christ-like. Thus we influence others like the leaven, and make them grow.

§ 3. *The Pictures of Eagerness and Self-Surrender*

Now, then, shut your eyes for the next pair of pictures. I see a labourer digging in the field, a poor man thinking about his poverty. Hour after hour he digs on patiently, stolidly; suddenly the spade strikes iron. "Hallo! some obstacle in the way," he says. He strikes it impatiently with the spade, smashes an old iron box thousands of years old, and out rolls a mass of flashing jewels and great gold coins. I see him dazzled and stunned, throwing himself upon it; then with a cry of delight, he puts back the earth, marks the spot, and rushes away home to his wife and children. "Oh! such a wonderful thing I have found! Let us sell the cow, and the sheep, and the cart, and our little house and land—aye, our furniture and clothes, and all that we have, to buy that field."

That picture is vanished. The scene changes. I see a travelling merchant with his little brown bag of pearls. He has been all over the country, seeking and buying. His bag is nearly full of precious stones. But he is not thinking of them. He is standing, rapt and astonished, before the noblest pearl that the world had ever seen— too grand for the crown of the mightiest king. "Oh! if I could get that, I should be a made man for ever." So he pours out his whole store that he had spent his all in buying. "Take them all! Take all I have! Only let me be the owner of that glorious pearl!"

What is the lesson? The glorious, priceless value of the Kingdom that Christ offers, and need of eager self-surrender in order to attain it. Christ says it is worth selling all that you have to get it. Why, of course it is! It satisfies all the cravings, and dissatisfactions, and ambitions which disturb people. It satisfies our whole nature, if we have really got hold of it. To be a member of Christ's Kingdom, living for Him, loving Him, helped and watched over by Him all my life, and then carried off to the eternal Kingdom to do beautiful, unselfish deeds in His presence, for ever and ever. If King Edward offered to put you all in beautiful palaces to-morrow, with all the money, and games, and bicycles, and holidays that your heart could desire, would it not be worth taking trouble, and giving up something to get it? Ah! children, some of us who are older have learnt that all these things we should soon tire of; and that for poor troubled sinners Christ's offer is ever so much grander and more desirable.

Can you get it? Can the poor heathen child get it? Not yet; the treasure is not yet hid in his field. The missionary must take it to him. But for every child within the Christian Church the treasure has been hid in his field since his Baptism. Some never find it, because they don't think of seeking it. Some come on it by chance, like the labourer. A mission time, or a chance sermon, or the words of a faithful friend, suddenly show what a precious treasure Christ has for them. They hardly deserve to find it, because they have not been seeking it. Why do they find it? Ah! because God has been seeking them, "seeking that which is lost, until He find it." Some, of nobler heart, are seeking and finding one little good after another. They are seeking goodly pearls, and to such God will surely see that they find at last the Pearl of Great Price. And then they cry, "Oh! what a blind fool I have been all my life, not to see how near my Lord was, and what a beautiful life He had for me." And they give up their whole life to Him in glad self-surrender. Pray to Him to teach you early, and not let you miss your treasure. Now read *vv.* 44-46.

§ 4. *The Pictures of What Shall Be at the End*

This time we read the parables *before* making the pictures. Read *vv.* 24-30, 36-43, 47-50.

Now it is your turn. One of you do the Tares picture for me. (Farmer sowing yellow wheat. Dark night. Enemy watching to do a spiteful trick. Stealthily creeping over wall to scatter his black tare-seed when all were trustingly asleep. The discussion in the later spring-time between master and servants, etc.) After the class have done this, let teacher do the Draw-net picture in same manner as before.

This pair of pictures is the answer to a puzzling question in men's minds. What? Yes. If all Christians within the Church were beautiful, lovable, unselfish characters, and all outside were wicked, and mean, and hateful, there would be no puzzle. It is just what we should expect, and would make people see much more plainly the value of Christ's Kingdom. Are they so? No; some Christians have grave faults, though they really care for and love Christ; and some godless people, who don't care about Christ, do some kind acts like Christians. So the good and bad seem so mixed that Christians are inclined to ask: "Lord, did not you sow all good seed? How have the tares crept in? Why have some Christian people faults of temper and carelessness, etc.?" What is the Lord's answer? (*v.* 28.) Is it the fault of His Gospel? No; but He says; "I have a terrible enemy—yours and Mine; and he hates to see Me pleased, or to see you happy. If we are happy, he is miserable; if we are sad, he is delighted. So he sows his black oats, and the tares get in to spoil My field."

This Sunday school is one of Christ's fields. Is it all pure, good wheat? Is each of you in this class so? Who has mixed up the tares with the wheat? Who has let the devil do it? Is it not a shame for us so to disappoint the Lord?

There are two important lessons in this pair of parables. What? First, *the patience of the Lord.* Why are the tares left? Because God is so kindly and merciful. Perhaps some will yet change into wheat. And, even if not, there is another reason? (*v.* 29.) Meaning? We are all so connected together in families and groups that you could not hurt one without hurting many. Just as in pulling up tares by the roots, you would disturb and pull up some wheat; so, if a father, or brother, or sister, were cast out now for being useless tares, many a true plant of Christ would be disturbed and injured.

But there is another reason why we should not be too eager to cast them out. And that is the second lesson of this pair of pictures. Because in the great Judgment time, God will infallibly sort them out. What do with wheat and tares? What with good and bad fish? So we should be very sorrowful for all who refuse to be

Christ's children. It will be awfully sad for them, when it is too late, to find that they have lost all. Everyone is now growing into what he shall be hereafter. And according to that shall the assortment take place. The Judgment must be according to character. All who can be *of no use* in God's beautiful Kingdom of unselfish life for others—all who are too mean, and selfish, and impure for that life—must be sent out into the outer darkness. Does God care? Is He troubled and pained at their going? Surely yes. And how are people made fit for the heavenly life? By surrendering their lives to Christ. He only can mould them into the life of love, and purity, and self-sacrifice, which shall be admitted into the Eternal Kingdom.

LESSON XII

AT CAESAREA PHILIPPI

St. Matthew XV. 21 to end, and XVI. to v. 23.

Last Sunday we thought of the seven pictures of
the Kingdom which our Lord showed. The next thing
that St. Matthew tells is the murder of John the Baptist,
and how John's disciples came and told Jesus about it.
He was evidently very sorry, and retired to a lonely
place; but the multitude followed Him, and followed
so far that they were out of the reach of food. So we
have the miracle of feeding the 5,000, and that same
night the Lord walking on the sea. We pass over all
these events, because they occur again in St. Mark's
Gospel, where we shall have Lessons about them. We
pass on then to *ch.* xv., where we find the priestly party
from Jerusalem beginning to disturb and oppose Him
(xv. 1), so that He has to withdraw off to the extreme
North, to the very border of the heathen land, near
Tyre and Sidon. Steadily, from this time forward, we
notice the hostile element increasing (xv. 1; xvi. 1, etc.),
the fickle crowds departing, the shadow of the Cross
deepening upon Him. It is the "beginning of the end."
From the time of the confession at Caesarea Philippi,

He began to teach the disciples of His coming death and resurrection (xvi. 21). After this feeding of the multitude comes the discourse in St. John vi., which resulted in many, even of His disciples, deserting Him (John vi. 66). So we have to keep in mind henceforth the sense of opposition and unpopularity in the minds of the Lord and His Apostles.

§ 1. The Canaanite Woman

Read xv. 21-31. Tired and persecuted, He withdrew to the far North. The city of Tyre, with its famous dyers and glass-workers; and Sidon, with its busy streets, its weavers, and brass-workers, and artists in precious stones, lay before Him; but He probably did not enter them. How do we know? (see *ch.* xi. 21.) Did not want to be noticed. "Don't tell people I am here," He says (St. Mark vii. 24).

But He could not be hid. The report of Him had already reached the North. One poor heathen woman had heard of His kindness, and sorely wanted help. Could not be kept back. She knew little of religion; but knew He was kind and powerful. "O Lord, save my little daughter. Cast out the devil." Bitter disappointment. Dead silence. Is He going to refuse? She struggles closer—"Lord, Lord, help me!" No use. He will not answer. Even the disciples plead for her, in order to get rid of her. What does He say? "Not meet to take," etc. Oh! how could He, so kind to others, be so harsh to her? What did He mean? Used the Jews' usual word of reproach for Gentiles—"dogs." Does she get up in a rage? "He called me a dog." Ah, no; she thought of the mad convulsions and horrible sufferings of her child, and she saw, too, something in His face not so cruel as His words. I think she saw His meaning better than many people to-day—not harshness, but simply stating the rule of the Gospel teaching, "To the Jew first, *and also* to the Gentile." She will humble herself to the dust. She will force Him by her earnestness. And as she thinks of the little dogs under the table, a brilliant thought comes. She will catch Him in His own words: "Not meet to throw it to the dogs." "Yes, Lord, it *is* meet to do it [see R. V.], for even the little dogs eat of the little children's crumbs." What did she mean? Who was the Master? Who the children at His table? Who the dogs? Yes. She thought of the Jews as the children in the Father's house, and she said: "Lord, let me be even as a little dog. I don't want to claim a child's part; but I will not leave the table until you throw me the dog's crumbs. Even if you spurn me or drive me away, I will still follow you. I terribly want your help. I have, at any rate, a dog's claim."

Wonderful faith. Wonderful humility. Wonderful love for her little girl. No longer could the Lord restrain Himself. "O woman," etc. (*v.* 28). Had He been unwilling before? Why so hard to her? We can only guess. Probably, for some wise reason, He had to confine Himself to Jews during His lifetime. Even in sending out disciples (*ch.* x. 5). Notice the sharp contrast which St. Matthew draws (see *vv.* 29-31), when He got back amongst Jews. Miracles then most freely performed. "And they glorified the God *of Israel.*"

Perhaps it was necessary to concentrate, just as one gathers together the embers into one hot fire, to warm whole place. So had this Kingdom of God to be kept together, concentrated, made powerful. But was it only for Jews' sake? No, but to make His Kingdom strong and powerful to reach the whole world afterwards. When did He give wider command? (St. Matthew xxviii. 19.) But probably His attitude here was for the woman's sake as well. He saw hers was a great soul, worthy of a great testing. He wanted to draw out and strengthen her faith. Must have been something in His look that kept up her faith all the time. Now she gained not only her daughter's cure, but a blessing for her own soul. He did not deal thus with other souls. Each soul treated in the way suited to it. *Teach here the power of intercessory prayer, and the lesson of faith, even when prayers not answered at once.*

§ 2. Feeding the Four Thousand

Read *vv.* 32-39. Notice the eager zeal of these people. Almost immediately afterwards they began to turn from Him. (See John vi. 66.) But as yet their enthusiasm remained. The Pharisees and priests had not yet succeeded in turning them against Him. Three days out with Him. Food all used up. He full of zeal for their good, teaching noble truths, healing and helping them. What a heavy, tiring strain on Him. Now He had compassion. On Himself? No, never thought of self, but only of others.

But He asks the disciples a curious question. Why

did He want their few little loaves? Could He not feed the crowd as well without them? Does He not do a far bigger miracle every year? What? Feeding the whole world at harvest. Why, then, ask for the few little brown loaves which the disciples had for their own supper? I think it was to teach a lesson to them and to us all. What? That it is by means of men He will help their fellow-men; that if you surrender to Him the little that you have for the sake of others, He will bless it, and increase it, and do vast good with it. E.g., a young clergyman or missionary, longing to help his fellows, feels: "I have but very little ability, or holiness, or power to help. Lord, I want the world helped, but I fear I can't do anything." The Lord says, as to the disciples, "How much have you? Bring it hither to Me; consecrate and surrender to Me that little, and I will bless it, and increase it, and help a whole multitude by it." So a boy or girl in school or family, or business. Always the question of Christ is coming to all who want to help their fellows: "How much have you? No matter how trivial or unimportant, bring it unto Me." So the weakest and stupidest is encouraged to help our Lord in His Kingdom. And often a boy or girl, or an ignorant poor person who loves the Lord, and wants to help the world, is used and blessed to do great good.

> "Whence shall we buy the bread to feed
> The hungry world's great growing need,
> When duties, thronging round us, wait
> Like suppliants around our gate?
> Whence shall we find our store of good,
> How give Thy waiting children food?
>
> "How many loaves have ye?"

"Ah! what avails our scanty store,
The few poor loaves upon our floor?
Wisdom wanting, faith grown old,
Doubtful knowledge, love grown cold;
So scant supplied, the hope were vain
Men's fainting spirits to sustain.

"Bring them hither to Me."

"We dare not send Thy guests away,
And bid them come another day.
Though poor the service we can give,
Thy touch can make the dead to live.
Take Thou our little, gracious Lord;
Place it upon Thy sacred board.

"And they did all eat."

"Then only when we yield to Thee
Our all, though small or great it be,
As duties grow, shall power grow more,
And all-sufficient be our store;
For not our zeal, or strength, or wit
For life's true service makes us fit.
Lord! lift Thy hand to consecrate,
And lo! our little groweth great."

§ 3. The Question at Caesarea Philippi

Notice again the Pharisees come to tempt Him and dispute with Him (xvi. 1), joining with their opponents the Sadducees for the purpose. Notice, too (*vv.* 5-12), how the disciples were unable to feel with Him or understand Him. One of the hard things of life to a sensitive nature such as His must have been this feeling of being alone without the keen sympathy

111

of friends who would understand and appreciate Him. See it again in *v.* 22. Even after all His high teaching about unselfishness and self-sacrifice, they could not understand why He should sacrifice His life for others.

Now (*v.* 13) we find them walking northward again to the gay little town of Caesarea Philippi, the fashionable resort of the rich people going for holidays in summer. But I don't think *they* came for holidays. I think there was a sad sense of opposition and unpopularity in the disciples' hearts as they followed Him while He taught. All their popularity and success dying away. Even their fellow-disciples deserting (John vi. 66). And I think the Lord's thoughts, too, were serious and solemn, though He would not feel discouraged, like the disciples. He was come to the last year of His life on earth, and He must soon go away, and leave that weak little band to conquer the world, and establish the Kingdom of God. And with such thoughts, as they sat, probably in view of the great rock, 1,000 feet high, which overhung the town, He breaks the silence with a question. What? I wonder if the disciples themselves were all very clear as to who He was. But, at any rate, they had listened to the talk of the people. What did the people think? Tell me anybody who thought He was John the Baptist? (*ch.* xiv. 2.) From Malachi's prophecy (Malachi iv. 5, 6), the rabbis thought that Elijah would come back again, and rise out of the middle of the Lake of Galilee. Like Tennyson's beautiful thought about King Arthur in the *Idylls of the King*. Others thought He was one of the prophets. What was disappointing in all this? That

112

no one seemed to recognise Him as the Messiah—the Christ—after all His time, and all His care, and love, and wonderful miracles. Was it not disappointing? Don't you think they all needed the encouragement of the two parables in last Lesson? Which two?

But there is another and more important question. Why more important? Because the whole future of the world's salvation depended on His little Church, which He should leave behind, being clear about this. What answer did He get? Was He pleased? I think *v.* 17 shows a delight and comfort in this bold statement. "These, after all, in spite of their stupid misunderstandings, do know who I am. Who has revealed it to them?" (*v.* 17.)

Don't you see, children, how everything depends on this? All the beautiful words and deeds of Christ would not do us much good, however we admired them, if He were only a good man. But when the poor, sinful, sorrowful world learns:—This is God who is showing this unselfishness, and kindness, and self-sacrifice for others; this is God's nature that is being shown to us; God has not forgotten us; He can't bear to let us perish; He loves us, and has given His very life for us;—don't you see what a splendid revelation that is for the poor world?

§ 4. *Peter the Rock-Man*

Tell me Christ's statement about Peter. I told you that right behind them was the great cliff-rock, one of the spurs of Mount Hermon. Perhaps our Lord thought of it as He spoke. And so glad was He of this strong faith

113

in Peter, that He tells him He would make him a great foundation-stone of His Church. You know how at the bottom of every building there are great foundation-stones; and often, at the beginning of building a church or great edifice, they lay the first of these, and call it *the* foundation-stone. So the Lord thinks of His Church as if it were a building of which the stones were living men.

Peter thinks of it thus also (see 1 Peter ii. 5), "Ye as living stones," etc. So also other writers in Scripture (see Ephesians ii. 20), "Built on the foundation of the apostles and prophets, Jesus Christ Himself being the chief cornerstone;" and Revelations xxi. 14, where the foundation-stones are "the twelve apostles of the Lamb." I think our Lord gave Peter a special honour amongst these foundation-stones. It was he who took the lead on the Day of Pentecost, when, at his preaching, the little "Kingdom of God" of 120 was increased by 3,000 (Acts ii. 41). It was he who was chosen to admit the Gentiles (Acts x.) into the Kingdom of God. So that, like as a man with a key, he was honoured to admit Jews and Gentiles into the Kingdom. It was a great honour, as Peter's was a great faith.

I should think Peter would be greatly troubled at the wrong use made of this honour in later days by the Church of Rome. When the city of Rome was the most important city of the world, the church existing in it would, of course, become the most important church in the world. But its clergy were not satisfied without inventing another reason for its greatness. Because this is the most powerful church, they said, there must be some Divine reason for it. And so, after hundreds of years, they declared that Peter had been the founder and bishop of their Church; and therefore they said that when the Lord gave Peter an honoured position, He meant that the Church of Rome should always have such an honoured position. And not only so, but that she should be supreme over all Churches, and her bishop should be over all bishops. Now, in reality there is no good reason to believe that Peter was ever Bishop of Rome at all; so that even if our Lord had given Peter supremacy over the other Apostles, and if He had said that this supremacy should belong to his successors in the city where he was bishop, it would be very difficult to attach that supremacy to Rome. But, as far as we can judge, no supremacy was given even to Peter himself. The other Apostles certainly did not think it. For (1) soon after this time there was a strife among them who should be the greatest; (2) James and John claimed the highest place in the kingdom; (3) Paul resisted Peter to the face, because he stood condemned (Galatians ii. 11); (4) the president of the first council was James, though Peter was present (Acts xv. 13). It seems pretty plain that neither Peter nor his comrades ever thought that the honour conferred on him carried such a supremacy; and as for the following words, "Whatsoever thou shalt bind," etc., we find that said to them all in *ch.* xviii. 18. We do not care to spoil our Lesson by further controversy. Suffice it, that the Lord gave a great honour to Peter. And all who share his faith and his grand avowal will, in their own degree, share in such honour of helping and building up the Kingdom of God.

§ 5. *Binding and Loosing*

This "binding and loosing" refers to *actions*, not to persons. It is "whatsoever," not "whosoever." If we judge by similar expressions in the Jewish literature, it seems to mean prohibiting or allowing actions, or, in other words, laying down the law of Christian conduct. Every community possesses this power. It is called the power of "public opinion." Even a school has that power. See how certain things are loosed or bound—i.e., allowed or prohibited by schoolboy public opinion, and scarce any boy dares to go against it. So in the army, cowardice is utterly disgraceful, because the strong public opinion of soldiers condemns it. A man who would not be ashamed of all the sins in the Decalogue feels utterly disgraced by the suspicion of cowardice. What schoolboys and soldiers bind and loose on earth may not always be bound and loosed in heaven, for they may not always be the right things that are bound or loosed by them.

But the Church, guided by the Holy Spirit, is placed here to form public opinion *for* righteousness and *against* unrighteousness. If the Church is true and fearless, that is a grand power over men, and Christ says that He will confirm it in heaven. So, when the nation adopts an unrighteous policy, or Parliament allows the great drink business to degrade the people, or when the general public sits still while the helpless classes are being wronged, it is the business of Christ's Church to rise in her Master's power to sternly denounce all such evil, and rouse a strong, righteous public opinion against it.

The Christian Social Union in England and in Ireland is an attempt to organize in the Church this great public opinion on the side of Righteousness. There is a terrible power on the other side. Rich and great and powerful people are interested in keeping up certain evils which are ruinous to the helpless classes. Take, for example, the great drink trade, which is sucking the life-blood out of the poor. Every city, every little country town, is swarming with drink-shops, and still new licences are being freely given, and temptations are being multiplied in every direction. Enormous fortunes are being made on the ruin of men's souls, and so great is the power of money that little can be done to prevent it. Indeed, the whole Christian conscience of this country to-day is unable to procure a law to keep little children out of the public-houses, though so many are anxious for it.

Whether it be unpopular or no, it is the Church's duty to bind and loose, to form public opinion according to God's will. More than once in her history she has fearlessly done so, e.g.:—when

> In Westminster's royal halls,
> Robed in their pontificals,
> England's ancient prelates stood
> For the people's right and good.
>
> Closed around the waiting crowd,
> Dark and still, like winter's cloud,

King and council, lord and knight,
Squire and yeoman, stood in sight;

Stood to hear the priest rehearse,
In God's name, the Church's curse.
By the tapers round them lit,
Slowly, sternly uttering it.

"Right of voice in framing laws,
Right of peers to try each cause;
Peasant homestead, mean and small,
Sacred as the monarch's hall,—

"Whoso lays his hand on these,
England's ancient liberties;
Whoso breaks, by word or deed,
England's vow at Runnymede;

"Be he Prince or belted knight,
Whatsoe'er his rank or might,
If the highest, then the worst,
Let him live and die accursed.

"Thou Who to Thy Church hast given
Keys alike of hell and heaven,
Make our word and witness sure,
Let the curse we speak endure!'

Silent while that curse was said,
Every bare and listening head
Bowed in reverent awe, and then
All the people said 'Amen'!"

It will be always a glorious day for the Church when she continues to represent the highest conscience of the community, and when, thrilled by the nobleness of her curse against wrong, all the people say, Amen!

ABOUT THE LITTLE ONES, AND ABOUT FORGIVENESS

St. Matthew XVIII.

§ 1. *About Christ's Little Ones*

Point out parallel passage, St. Mark ix. 33. Remember last Sunday's story of Caesarea Philippi. We have omitted the seventeenth chapter, which tells of Transfiguration, as it is taught fully in the St. Mark Lessons. After the Transfiguration they went on through Galilee, and came to Capernaum (xvii. 24; Mark ix. 30).

On the road the Lord overheard a dispute going on behind Him. They thought He had not heard. He knows all our thoughts and words. Utterly confused and ashamed, when, as they sat in the house, He quietly turned to ask them—what? Felt like school-boys caught in some wrong that they thought was not known. Already had learned enough to be ashamed of dispute. What was it about? Why this dispute now? Perhaps because, Peter, James, and John chosen to be at Transfiguration. Perhaps the high praise given to

Peter at Caesarea Philippi. This account in St. Matthew begins: "Who, *then*, is greatest?" (see R.V.). The "then" makes one think that there has been previous talk of it. Perhaps they think, if we may not *dispute*, at any rate we may *inquire*. So they ask, "Who, then, is greatest?" But the whole discussion shows how totally they misunderstood the beautiful self-sacrifice which He was always trying to teach them—showed a selfish, earthly spirit. The Lord was sorry to see this bad spirit. Tried to teach them the law of greatness of the Kingdom of Heaven—what? (*v.* 4.) Meaning? THE HIGHEST GREATNESS IN GOD'S SIGHT IS THAT OF HUMBLING AND FORGETTING SELF FOR THE SERVICE OF OTHERS. THE LOWEST POSITION IN GOD'S SIGHT IS HIS WHO IS ONLY STRIVING AND STRUGGLING FOR HIS OWN GAIN AND GREATNESS. All class repeat this. Take case of boy or girl at home. Describe to me the sort that will be highest or lowest in God's sight. Take case of merchant, politician, etc. By such questioning into details, make the subject real and practical to the children.

How did He begin teaching this lesson? Called to Him a little child, perhaps one of Peter's small boys, as this was probably Peter's house in Capernaum (Mark ix. 33). Did the child come? Yes. I think any child who knew Him would have run to Him. I can imagine the boy, in his little striped tunic, with bare arms and legs, running to Him at once. Don't you think the children in that house would be fond of the Lord Jesus, who often came in amongst them? Do you think children soon find out who is fond of them? Some people don't care for children. Some greatly love them—which sort our

Lord? Did he tell the little chap to stand away from Him while He taught this lesson? What then? Lifted him on his knee; put His arms around him (Mark ix. 36). I don't think He could help doing that whenever He got a little child near Him (see Mark x. 16). He was so fond of them, they could not help being fond of Him. You could not either, if you saw Him and knew Him, as you will one day in heaven. He was very popular with children. They ran to Him, clung to Him in His arms, shouted "Hosanna" to Him. What a kindly friend for children! Full of sympathy for their innocent pleasure and mirth. Children cling to Him; don't disappoint Him.

Think of these eager, grasping apostles, each worrying and striving to be greater than the others. See them looking at this innocent little child taken from his play, and wondering in his little heart how he came to be taken such notice of. No thought in *his* mind about their wretched strivings and ambitions. Quietly nestling in the arms of Jesus; living in the present, not fretting about the future, he is just the example to teach them Christ's lesson: "Unless ye become like this child." How? Does it mean that child sinless? Or any child? Tradition—This child was afterwards the great martyr, St. Ignatius, thrown to wild beasts in Rome. Perhaps true. Probably fond enough of our Lord to die for Him. But surely not sinless. All mankind fallen. Even little children need a Saviour. But the Lord wanted to teach child-like spirit. Children, unless badly brought up, are innocent, contented, kindly—not self-conscious, not supercilious, or making class distinctions. Not fretting about the future. Peacefully, quietly trusting their parents, and living just "one day at a time." The hard world hardens and spoils us. The Lord says, "Keep the child-like heart in you. Be as little children in the Great Father's home. Not worrying or fretting for greatness, but loving and trusting the Father, and gladly doing His will." What is the secret of the child being so happy and child-like? *He is sure that he is loved.* Our first great lesson to learn in God's service is that. Be sure that you are loved, more than by parent or dearest friend. That is a more important lesson even than to learn that you are sinful. Nothing helps us like feeling that we are loved and cared for. That makes us "like little child."

Watch Him still with child clasped in His arms. "Whoso receiveth," etc. (*v.* 5). One *such* little child. I think it means not children only, but any humble follower of His who had become "like a little child." But, of course, it includes the little children too, and, in St. Mark's account, little children especially. How He loved children, and commended them to men's care. But, oh! how angry if one led them wrong! What does he threaten? (*v.* 6.) Meaning of "offend"? Think of Him looking at the little boy, and letting His thoughts run on into future, when people should tempt that child away from God. How awful Christ's anger! Shows how great His love for children. Show me how this anger could be deserved, (1) by parent or teacher; (2) by one of you. Worst sin in God's sight is to tempt another to do wrong.

Meaning of verses 8, 9. Tell us to cut off hand or foot with knife? What then? If tooth very bad—no rest or sleep—what do? Pull it out. Painful? Yes; but worse evil to leave it in. Whatever habit, or companionship, or occupation causes you to stumble, away it must be cast, even if as dear as right hand or eye. Tell me some such? Desire for drink; wicked companion, who is pleasant; occupation or amusement dangerous to modesty or truthfulness, etc. However painful, cut it off. Better to suffer—better to die—than to sin. So the Lord says, and He should know. How awful sin must appear to Him!

He says one very wonderful thing at the end, to make people feel the enormous importance of the children (*vv.* 10-12). Meaning: I think it means that we have all guardian angels in special charge of us, and that the little children's angels are the closest to God's throne. I suppose that nearness to the throne means that children are especially precious in God's sight. I don't wonder. They have not yet got spoiled or hardened, and, if they will only let God keep them close to Him, they have such a beautiful future before them. But if they stray from God, then does He get tired of them, and give them up? (*v.* 12.) Why? Because *v.* 14. Is it not an awful shame if any of them persist in going away from Him?

§ 2. *About Forgiving People*

Read *vv.* 15-35. Now the wee boy is off to his play again, feeling, probably, that he, too, must be kinder and gentler to his little comrades in future. And the conversation goes on—about what? Did anybody ever do anything against you? Think for a moment, and tell me some of them that you remember. You need not tell *who* did it, but what? Now, what does our Lord tell you to do to him if he is sorry? Forgive. But if he is not sorry? Are you then to go and sulk about it? Are you to go about and tell all your acquaintances about it? What then? (*v.* 15.) Forgiveness is not much good to him if he is not sorry; but the *forgiving spirit* must be in your heart. First make sure whether you may be in any degree to blame yourself. If so, go to him and say: "I'm afraid I began this—I'm sorry." Any generous boy or girl would respond to that at once, and confess his own wrong; and so you would have done him good, and kept him from sin, and pleased the Lord. In any case, you are to feel sorry for him if you are sure that he is in the wrong, and not penitent. And if you can do anything to bring him right, do it. If necessary, ask one or two friends to speak to him—very few. Always keep it as private as possible. The rest of the advice is rather for big people, and we may pass over it.

But Peter is a bit puzzled by this. It looks as if you might go too far with this forgiveness. So he asks— what? The Jewish Rabbis said, "Until three times," but he thought Jesus might want more than that. What is the Lord's answer? Does that mean exactly 490 times? No; it is His way of saying, "Whenever one comes to you, sorry for a wrong, you must *always*, without any exception, forgive him from your heart."

And then He tells them a parable that should force any man to forgive. Tell it me very carefully—every point is important. Now for meaning. Who is the King? What is the reckoning? No. I think not the Day of Judgment, else how could the rest of parable happen? Sometimes God's Holy Spirit makes one feel one's sin deeply—reckons it up to him, like a kind creditor, who wants to save one from going too much in debt. This sinner asks God—what? No, not to let him off, but give him time. He thinks he can pay off his debt by being good in future. Can he? He is bound to be good in future, any way; and what of his past? What does God do? Forgave it all. Why? Because man could not pay. Moved with compassion. Fancy forgiving a huge debt like that—more than a million pounds. That means that every one who is neglecting God's service, and using God's gift for evil or for selfishness, owes a tremendous debt to God.

Try to see this. Often dying men tell me, when I say this to them, "Oh, I have not done much harm in my life." And therefore they feel satisfied. But, don't you see, God puts us here, not merely to keep from doing harm, but to do good: to make life a noble, lofty, beautiful thing for ourselves and others. Fancy God saying to you, "My child, I have given you health, and strength, and cleverness, and friendships, and a happy home, and influence with your comrades, etc., etc., because I want you to help Me to make this poor old world good. Now, what have you done for Me?" And you say, "Well, Lord, I think I have not done much harm!" Do you think that would do? Why, a rabbit or a pig could give as good an account as that—"I have not done much harm." Fancy saying, "Well, Lord, I'm as good as a rabbit or a pig, at any rate." What a proud boast, after all God's splendid gifts to you, given to be used for good. People don't see that this sin of theirs is great, like the debt of 10,000 talents. But in eternity it will be quite plain. Look round this room. You don't see that the whole air is full of motes. But a strong sunlight shows it at once. So with the light of God. If any of you neglect to live the beautiful, righteous life, your debt is not yet as bad as the whole 10,000 talents, for you have not yet wasted very much. Don't feel frightened at it, as if life were all a task-work. God wants it to be a very happy life. But you should think of it if you have been forgetting Him, and go and ask Him to forgive you. Will He? And whenever you understand how great and full is God's forgiveness, you will be so touched by it that you can never be unforgiving to another. You would feel as mean as the man in the parable. Is there anything that could ever make him withdraw that forgiveness? (*v.* 35.) What then is the rule of forgiveness? Even as God for Christ's sake hath forgiven you. What does the Lord's Prayer and what does the Litany bid us pray about forgiveness?

LESSON XIV

MAKING BARGAINS
WITH GOD

St. Matthew XIX. 16 to end, and XX. to v. 17.

§ 1. The Great Refusal

Read *ch.* xix. 16-22. Then glance at account in St. Mark x., noticing the "running" and "kneeling," and that Jesus was so attracted by him that He "beholding him loved him." This is an example of Christ's attitude towards sincere earnestness of purpose, which yet was not a strong enough purpose. See what a kindly, sympathetic attitude. How He believed, and sympathized with, and liked the young ruler, and determined to run a big risk in order to make a man of him.

He must have been greatly impressed by Christ, afraid he might miss his chance, now that He was leaving the neighbourhood. So came running to Him. What do you think of him? Good? Yet with a deep feeling that all was not right, that he lacked something. What? Right desires? Earnestness? Humility? Belief in God? No. (Let children prove that he had all these.)

127

Like doctor probing and questioning, Christ treats him to find out for him his lack. What direction does He give? (*v.* 17.) Young man asks, What commandments? Surely not the ordinary Ten Commandments that I know? What does Jesus reply? Yes. But could this man, or any man, keep them perfectly? Yet the effort to keep them is the truest way to find the power—to find Christ. No real, true life without obedience. In proportion as men tried to obey the old law, so were they pleasing to God, and so were they ready to receive Christ, and the fuller power which He would bring. In proportion even as the poor heathen obey God's law in their conscience, and try to do the little right they know, in that proportion are they ready to receive Christ when truly presented to them. "He that *willeth to do*, he shall know" (John vii. 17).

The young ruler rather impatiently replies—what? Had he really kept them? Why did he think so? See Lesson IV, and Christ's fuller teaching as to the high demands of commandments rightly understood. This young man did not know all this, which every Sunday School child knows now. Therefore, he thought that the outward keeping from gross sins was all that was needed. Is it? Surely not. True hearts, who know God's will, and are striving after it, the more they strive to do it perfectly, the more they see how unable they are to succeed. But we must not wonder at this young man with his very imperfect knowledge.

Did Jesus at once rebuke him angrily for his conceit and spiritual pride? (Mark x. 21.) Ah! no. He was touched with his simplicity and honesty. He looked into his heart, saw his striving for better things—his desire for highest, noblest life. Then, with His great love for him, He saw that only one terrible test would show him his lack. It was an awfully hard test for a rich, prosperous young man, the favourite of the world. "Give up all, and become a beggar, and follow Me!" Is that command for every man—sell everything, and be a beggar? No; it is His will for some, and some have nobly done it. It is His will that every one of us *should be ready* to give up all for Him. But He does not demand that all should do it. Abraham, David, many of His servants were rich. But He saw it was the one thing wanted to make a splendid fellow of this young ruler. Like a surgeon risking dangerous operation, the only chance for his patient. Would it have been worth giving up all to follow Christ? What would he have got in exchange? The joy of self-sacrifice—of religion—of the favour and approval of Christ, and, therefore, of his own conscience. In a few months after hundreds did it (Acts iv. 34-37). He was just on the brink of gaining all this, and being happy for ever. The Lord watched him. What would he do? His eternal life depended on it. Alas! he failed (*v.* 22). But also he learned his lack of real religion. His question was answered. But with what feelings did he go away? May we not hope that he came back again to Christ! Surely he could never be satisfied again with his money and his fine house, apart from Christ!

At any rate, he went away, and Christ let him go. And the disciples learned again the great lesson that the true follower after Christ must be willing to give up all rather than lose Him. This sets Peter thinking, and he asks—what? Was there anything wrong in asking this? Think carefully. Suppose you asked that same question of your mother when she wanted your help? I don't think the Lord liked Peter's tone, and I think that was why He told the parable.

§ 2. *Men Who Don't Make Bargains with God*

Read the parable very carefully, *noticing especially what agreements the different labourers made.* Now, children, try and guess the meaning. What do you think of these guesses that I have read? (1) That everyone should have equal rewards, no matter whether they joined the kingdom as little children or in old age? I don't think that is God's way at all: besides see xix. 30; xx. 16. (2) That it means that length of time does not matter, but earnestness of work? Do you think that is it? Surely not, for the parable does not say anything about the later ones working more earnestly than others.

To find meaning, go back to Peter's question. What was wrong in it? Yes. Well, I think this parable is the rebuke to it, and that it is to teach the difference between work done for sake of reward, in a bargaining spirit, and work done for love of God and of the work, and leaving all question of reward to the loving, generous God who appointed the work. E.g., you have heard something of the poverty, and misery, and overcrowding, and disease in the slums of our cities. Now, suppose the Church in her Synods, called for volunteers to help in this work by endeavouring to remove these evils; suppose a hundred workers volunteer; suppose that some who work hard and well are thinking of reward or popularity, etc. "This is a popular work; we like being connected with it," etc. They do good work, but not entirely for love of God or the poor, but partly for love of themselves. Others have their hearts so sore with trouble for the poor women and little children that they never think of what they shall get—never think of themselves at all. "Oh, let me do anything to help—run messages, sweep offices; any work that may never be praised or heard of; anything to help God in relieving these poor children of His out of their wretchedness." Which class would you think most of?

Now, that is pretty much the position here. For what does Christ call us into His Kingdom on earth? To help to make this poor old world happier and better. It is full of sin, and misery, and selfishness. The heart of our Lord is sore as He looks at it, and He is, as it were, all day hiring His helpers, trying to get men in to work in His vineyard. Was Peter helping? Yes, from the very beginning of the work. But his question showed that he was thinking a good deal of rewards—either a high place on earth, or perhaps a high distinction in heaven. Could this sort of man do good work? Yes; but not the best sort. Not like the man who would say, with full, generous trust, "Lord, just let me in; give me a chance to help Thee to relieve the sin and misery of life, and do what seemeth good with me then." Even the worker whose work is not quite unselfish will get a reward (*v.* 29), a hundredfold. No work for God is ever unrewarded. But it is those who work for love

131

of Christ, and of their poor brethren, not merely for reward, who are dearest to His heart, and will receive the highest blessing.

§ 3. Hiring in the Market-Place

Now we are in a better condition to understand the parable. Picture it to yourselves as it might happen in any country town at harvest time. Labourers in the market-place at harvest time, waiting to be hired. Early morning. Farmers walking along the ranks, choosing their men. One great householder wants a large number. They ask, "What will you pay? We can get four or five shillings a day from Mr. A. What will you give?" *And so he makes an agreement with them to pay a certain price* (*v.* 2), and sends them to work.

By-and-by he walks through market-place again; 12 o'clock, 3 o'clock, even as late as 5 o'clock in the evening, and still some are waiting, tired and dispirited. Why not working? (*v.* 7.) Farmer A, and B, and C are there looking for cheap bargains. "I'll give you a bit of food, at any rate, if you work for rest of the day. Better you should get that than nothing." But the great, kind householder hates to see the poor fellows cheated. "Men, you know me. I have plenty of work for you, and *whatsoever is right,* that shall ye receive." *They make no bargains.* They know he can be trusted. They are touched by his kind thought for them; they know he is a generous, large hearted man; and they work with *heart,* with *feeling,* though only for a few hours. This pleases him. It would please anybody. A mistress has a servant who works well, but keeps rigidly to her carefully drawn-up agreement as to her hours, and her days off, and her pay, etc. She has another servant, who gets fond of her and fond of the children; and if mistress is tired, or one of the children sick, never thinks of her day off or her privileges, but sits up at night, and does what she can to make things comfortable, never asking if she will get extra pay. Which of the two would be likely to get well rewarded?

Now describe the scene at the paying of the men. Don't you think it would rebuke Peter's question? I don't think Christ's true followers would be really as envious as this. But this is a warning to show the ugliness of Peter's question. Who are those who went to work in morning? Children. Who at 3 o'clock and 5 o'clock? Those who had wasted much of their lives. Do you think, then, from this parable, that it is best to be of the second sort? Ah! no; the people who come into Christ's vineyard late are always sad and sorry for the lives they have wasted, saying, What a pity I did not come in as a child! Do you think that *all* who come in early have the selfish, bargaining spirit? Or *all* who come late, the trustful, unbargaining spirit? No, indeed; some of each may come in either mood. But all my experience shows me that the truest and most loving workers in the great vineyard of Christ came in as little children. Children, remember how the Lord is discouraged looking for workers who will not come. And the poor wretched old world is still going wrong and still very full of misery and sin. Think of it. Say to Him, "O Lord, take me, and let me help. Do just what is best with me afterwards;

only let me help Thee. I'm not a bit afraid to trust Thee with my future. Whatever Thou doest will be a thousand times more than I deserve; but, at any rate, take me. Let me help."

GOING UP TO JERUSALEM TO DIE

St. Matthew XX. 17 to end, and XXI. to v. 17.

We are at "the beginning of the end." We come to-day to one of the last stages—the sorrowful journey to Jerusalem to die. All the remaining Lessons are little more than the story of Holy Week, the story of the Cross and Passion. So from this time forward the Lessons take a sadder and more solemn tone.

§ 1. *The Last Journey*

Read *vv.* 17-28. Read also Mark x. 32-45. The road to Jerusalem crowded with people going up to keep the Passover; family groups picking up their friends on the way; pilgrims from afar on camels and horses; country people on asses or on foot; pedlars with their wares, fruit-sellers with their baskets—a great, bustling crowd, pressing on to Jerusalem. One group by itself, looking troubled and perplexed; and away in front of them their lonely Leader, with the firm resolve in His heart, and the glory of self-sacrifice so apparent in His face that a great awe has fallen on His followers. "They were amazed," St. Mark says, "and as they followed they were afraid." They could not yet understand the glory of the self-sacrificing life.

They evidently had a notion that a crisis of some sort was near. Perhaps they thought the great crowd in Jerusalem, in their excited enthusiasm, would now rise against the Romans, and make Him a king, and bring in the kingdom. Perhaps the people on the road showed signs of this feeling. Perhaps it was through fear of their encouraging some foolish rising that He called His disciples apart to tell them something very solemn and sad. What? (*vv.* 18-20.) Should not you think they would be heart-broken by this news? I can't understand them unless that they felt pretty sure that things would end better than He expected—that the people would give Him a crown instead of the cross that He looked for.

Poor foolish friends! They thought that the little, petty crown of Judea, and glory, and comfort, and praise for Himself, would be dearer to Jesus than His great purpose of sacrificing Himself for men. You see, the Holy Ghost had not yet come in full power into the world, and it was harder for men to rise into great high thoughts like His. But, all the same, it must have made it very lonely for Him that no one amongst His closest friends could feel with Him or understand Him. Their thoughts and hopes were of lower and meaner things.

§ 2. The Sons of Zebedee

Tell me about the mother of Zebedee's sons. Was it not disappointing? Such low thoughts. "The kingdom is to be established. It is full time for us to be looking after the high places in it." I like to think that it was not James and John themselves, but their mother. It is so like a mother—everything for her sons; nothing for herself. That is the good side of it.

But the bad is very bad. They and Peter were the Lord's closest friends. They thought, because they were His relatives, that they could oust Peter, and come behind backs to ask special favour for themselves. And this, after all His beautiful life and teaching about self-sacrifice—after being told that he was going up that day to sacrifice Himself for others. Don't you think the Lord would feel lonely and disappointed? What does He say? (*v.* 22.) Meaning of this? Did they know that He meant suffering? Yes; He had just told them (*v.* 18). What did they reply? So they were brave fellows, and willing to suffer for Him; but they wanted to be put highest in glory above the others. If they had really Christ's spirit in them, what would the request be? "Lord, grant us to serve, to be of use in Thy Kingdom, even if it be in the lowliest place." Was the Lord vexed? No. He saw the good in them, as well as the evil. He knew that in the days to come they, like Himself, would know the glory of self-sacrifice. So He answered kindly. Did He promise the thrones? What? (*v.* 23.) Pain—self-sacrifice—death for sake of Christ and Gospel. These He thought better for them than thrones without Him. One day they, too, thought it. For the Lord's prophecy was fulfilled—how? James executed (Acts xii. 2). John exiled and martyred.

Still more disappointment? (*v.* 24.) Why indignant? Did the Lord notice it? Yes. Think how disappointing to Him, with all His noble, beautiful thoughts, to have as his closest companions men who could not enter into His feelings at all. Here were they again disputing. Same disease of ambition and self-seeking was in them all. See how kindly He bears with them. Think how His words should draw out all that was good in them. "True greatness," He says, "such as I am following, is to be reached by the way of humility and the lowly service of others. I came to earth not to be"—what? Meaning of "to minister"? The ambition of men is to have many servants—the ambition of Christ was? To serve. Motto of the Princes of Wales, "I serve." What a glory it would give their lives if really followed their motto as Christ did. That was the glory He sought; and He goes on to tell the very height of that glory—what? "And to give His life." What a lovely world heaven must be when that is the object of aim and ambition. To serve others. To give His life for others. Pray: "Lord, help me to understand Thee, to adore Thee, to follow Thee in my own lowly way in the ambition of service."

§ 3. Palm Sunday in Jerusalem

By this time they had come to Jericho, the beautiful city of palm-trees, where a great crowd gathered around, and where one little man, who was so anxious to see Him, climbed up into a tree, as I saw boys do lately in

Dublin when the Queen was passing. Who was he? (St. Luke xix. 2.) More and more the crowd increased, till it was almost like a royal procession, as the Lord left Jericho. Then He healed the two blind men, and, I dare say, did many other miracles as He went on, until they arrived, tired and footsore, at Lazarus' house in Bethany, probably on the Friday evening before Palm Sunday. (Before the beginning of *ch.* xxi. you must insert His arrival at Bethany.)

In that Bethany home Jesus spent His last Sabbath (*ch.* xxvi. 6; John xii. 1); and the next day, Sunday, which we now keep as Palm Sunday, was the first day of the week of the Passion. Now comes a curious change in His whole attitude. Up to this we have read of His retiring from notice, of His forbidding people to tell of His cures, of His general desire to avoid unnecessary publicity. Now we have the very opposite. He is actually arranging for a public procession into Jerusalem, just when the whole place is full of excited crowds at the Passover feast. Evidently He has some great purpose in view. Does He want to escape the Cross, and be carried off by the enthusiastic crowd to be made king in the palace at Jerusalem? Surely not. For what has He told His disciples? (xx. 18.) He has come up to die. But before He dies, He must make a last appeal to the nation, whose chief representatives are now up at Jerusalem at the feast. The nation must have one more chance of accepting Him before it is too late.

Tell me about His arrangements? (xxi. 1-4.) Does not it show that He was a King? Without any spies He could see what was at Bethphage; without any army He could make men obey His bidding (*vv.* 2-4). He could know everything and do everything. His procession was not a very grand one. Not stately horses and chariots, and guards of soldiers, like the processions in the Queen's visit to Ireland lately. Just a young Galilean teacher riding on an ass, the symbol of peace, and with a shouting crowd behind Him. Would it mean anything to the Romans in Jerusalem? Why should it be so impressive to the Jews? Because the Jews knew by heart the chief prophecies about the Messiah; and almost every Jew who saw Jesus that day would think of the famous prophecy in Zechariah. Read it for me. Remember there was already wild excitement about Him. The people on all sides had heard of His miracles. A crowd had gone out to Bethany the day before to see Him, and see Lazarus, whom He had raised up (John xii. 9). All men were asking whether He was the Messiah. So this is His public claim, His public assertion, "I *am* the Messiah; I am the Christ who was to come."

Did the crowd believe Him? Yes. In no other way can we explain that wild enthusiasm that stirred the whole city. They flung their clothes on the ground for Him to ride over; they tore down palm-branches to strew in the way. They shouted with eager excitement the words that could only mean welcome to the Messiah. For the time, at least, that huge crowd of people in Jerusalem believed that Jesus was the promised Messiah. It was a great day for Jerusalem. For the moment it almost seemed as if they would recognise their King, and yield themselves to the beautiful life of unselfish devotion to which He called them. It is a very wretched thing to go near to accepting Christ as our King, and then to stop short. Many boys and girls do. I think it is a very sad thing to look at that multitude so enthusiastic on Sunday, and to see them all the rest of the week rejecting the Lord. And a very sad thing, too, to think of a Sunday School class like this, learning about Jesus now, interested in the story, and some of them in their later days going away from Him altogether. I don't like to discourage you, but I want to warn you. I have known bright, pleasant boys and girls who once seemed to care for the Lord, but who are now, I fear, utterly gone from Him. Pray to Him that it may not be so with you.

Now tell me of His triumphal visit to the Temple? Like a king coming back to his own house, left in the charge of caretakers, and indignantly rebuking them for their neglect. Think of your parish church always as the House of God left in the charge of caretakers by Him. Who are the caretakers? The parishioners. When you are grown up, be very careful about your parish church, that its worship shall be bright, and beautiful, and pure from error; that the building itself and its surroundings shall be kept as the King's house should be—nothing slovenly or unbecoming.

Something about children at the close of this story? I think He was always glad of children's love especially, He was so fond of children. I wonder if some of you will give Him pleasure by loving and being faithful, when many older people are neglecting and disappointing Him.

LESSON XVI

WARNINGS IN THE TEMPLE

St. Matthew XXI. 18 to end.

Notice distinctly that we have now come to the week of the Passion, the last week of our Lord's life on earth. Last Lesson told of the triumphal entry on Sunday. We now go on to the rest of the week. Notice, still the change in His attitude. All must now be public and open, and courting, rather than avoiding, notice. No longer doing good deeds quietly, and telling men to keep silent about them. No longer avoiding conflict with the authorities. It is full time now to bring matters to an issue. This week brings the crisis of the fate of the nation. They must be made now, in full, clear consciousness, to accept or reject Him. It must be made impossible to ignore or overlook Him any longer.

§ 1. *The Withered Fig-Tree*

Read *vv.* 18-22. What morning? Monday. But for *v.* 20 see Mark xi. 20, where you learn that this surprise of the disciples was on next morning, Tuesday. Why did He destroy fig-tree? Was it not strange to act thus towards

142

a senseless tree? Why do you think He did it? Perhaps meant partly to show His power; but especially meant, I think, as an acted parable to teach a terrible lesson. This fig-tree was a symbol of Jewish Church (Hosea ix. 10). Now guess the teaching? Yes, the subsequent parables quite bear this out. He had seen from heaven this Jewish Church with its great professions of religion, like the beautiful deceptive leaves, with no fruit beneath them. He now indicates the stern anger of God at such empty profession.

There is another lesson also in *v.* 21. What? The great power of facing difficulties with strong faith in God. Never mind how utterly impossible an undertaking may seem: if it is right and needed, and according to God's will, face it confidently, though it seem as hopeless as casting the mountain into sea. Does it mean that you could make a literal mountain fall into the sea? I remember when a child commanding a mountain to do so. But, alas! the mountain never stirred; and though I am afraid I had hardly expected it to stir, yet this verse puzzled me. We Western people are very prosaic, and don't understand Eastern poetical way of saying things. Disciples would quite understand what our Lord meant, that the man with strong faith in God could command things that looked as impossible as this.

§ 2. *Conflict with the Priests*

This Tuesday a terrible day of strain and conflict. Turn over leaves of Bible from this to end of *ch.* xxv. All these things happened on Tuesday, and other things, too, recorded by other evangelists. Don't you think there would have been to Him terrible weariness and nerve-strain after it? When He came to Temple this Tuesday morning, who met Him? Of course they were very angry. Remember Jerusalem crowded with people for Passover. Temple crowded. He had dared to turn out buyers and sellers, to do miracles, to teach publicly in Temple. What do they ask? Do you see any trap in this question? Probably expected Him to say He was God, and then could charge Him with blasphemy. Did He? No. "Before answering," said He, "I should like your opinion about something." What? Why was this difficult? (*vv.* 25-27.) But what had this to do with their question about His authority? Don't you see? (1) All held John to be a prophet inspired of God. (2) John had borne witness to Christ. He said: "I am nobody— only a voice in the wilderness. I have only come to prepare the way of the Lord. He that cometh after me is mightier" (Matthew iii. 11-12). "Behold," cried he, pointing to Jesus—"behold the Lamb of God" (John i. 29-36). Therefore, if they said John's mission was from Heaven, He would reply, "Why, then, do ye not believe his statement that I am the Messiah?" So you see why they dared not answer. Therefore He would not answer them. Did they deserve an answer? Why not? If they had been true, earnest men, who were in doubt about Him, would He have treated them thus? Surely not.

§ 3. *The Two Sons*

Tell me this parable. Of course it was aimed at the audience before Him. Who was the certain man? What classes meant by the two sons? The first think themselves very religious, talk about God and religion, and go to church, etc.; but *do* nothing of God's work. Second class, the openly irreligious, who did not at all profess to do God's work until something touched them, and they "repented and went." Which class did the priests belong to? How did He make them condemn themselves?

What is the lesson of this parable for us? That our WORK is the important thing, not our thinkings or feelings. If we are not DOING anything to help to make life happier and holier for others, it is no excuse to say we like going to church, or that we wish we were better, or that we admire unselfishness, and think it very lovely. The world is full of sin and trouble, and social misery. When you get bigger, you will find Temperance and Missionary and Social Service work, and religious work of every kind, waiting to be done, and being largely left to clergy to do. When you see that, it is a call of God to you, "Son, go work in my vineyard." But what can you do in vineyard now? Learn lessons well, and so prepare for future usefulness. Help to make school life and home life pure and unselfish. Be brave enough to stand out against comrades if anything mean, or false, or impure is being said or done, etc. All this is work in God's vineyard. He is so wanting to make a noble, beautiful world, and He likes to let us all help.

§ 4. The Wicked Husbandmen

What sort of mood do you think the chief priests and elders are in now? Very angry? Yes; but also, I think, a little bit cowed and subdued. All their imperious domineering had failed, and with the crowd listening and, I suppose, enjoying it, they had to stand silent, and listen like children to His stern teaching. He had been so gentle always before, that they hardly know Him now. Like a lion roused, something in His look and manner awes them. So, before they can recover from rebuke (*vv.* 31, 32), He turns on them again. "Here another parable." Tell me this parable accurately. Who was householder? Vineyard? Jewish people. Out of the great wilderness of the sinful world God had, as it were, walled off one corner, where the plants should be specially tended and cared for. Were Jews more tended and taught than other nations? Yes. No other nation on earth got such care, and teaching, and help of every kind to be religious. Was this because they were special pets and favourites, and that God did not care much for the others? Certainly not. Impress on children that it was *for the sake of all the rest* that the Jews were trained, that they might preserve and hand down religion through all the world. This is most important. The idea of God's favouritism for some peoples and neglect for others must never be entertained.

What should have been the result of all this care? Was it so? No, Jews thought they were God's special pets, and instead of trying hard to be deeply religious, and so help others to be so, they were content with listening to the prophets, and reading the Bible, and going to church, and not *doing* anything. Just like a vineyard absorbing all the water and manure, etc., into the soil, and bearing no fruit.

Did God really go away? (*v.* 33.) Where else does Christ say the same thing? (Matthew xxv. 14.) What does it mean? Not *really* absent—is near to everyone who wants to be helped; but His visible presence and miracles, etc., withdrawn, so that men should feel free to act as they thought best. Who were the servants? Prophets, good kings, etc. What did God send them for? (*v.* 34.) *Fruits.* What does it mean? Yes; just the same as in Parable of Two Sons. Fruits of a good, true, beautiful life, which God sought. How treated? (*v.* 35.) (See also Matthew xxiii. 34; Jeremiah xxxv. 15; Acts vii. 52, etc.)

Now comes something very touching (*v.* 37). Why touching? Because He was talking with calm sadness of what He knew would be done to Himself in a few days. Does He put Himself down as one of the servants, merely a prophet like other prophets? No. The Son—the Son of God. Though so gentle and modest always, He never drops this claim. And He seems to say, too, "This is God's final and greatest message." Last of all, He sent His Son, as if He would say: "God has no more now that He can do. He has made His last move. He has no other messenger, no other inducement. If men will not be touched by that, their case is hopeless." Show me again how He makes the priests condemn themselves. Notice the simile of the great Foundation Stone, which now lies in the way of all men to be built upon. And if they will, like negligent builders, leave it about unused, they will fall on it, and hurt themselves. All who know about Christ and try to ignore Him will surely hurt their souls. But there is always a chance of remedying this until the end, when it is too late, and the Christ whom they have ignored and neglected shall come in judgment, like a great stone falling on the wicked.

LESSON XVII

ENEMIES LAYING SNARES FOR HIM

St. Matthew XXII. omitting vv. 23-34.

Remember last Lesson. Keep in mind that we are in the week of the Betrayal and Crucifixion; that the Lord is in stern conflict with the Pharisees; that ever since Palm Sunday He has been making high claims, and administering severe rebukes. Last Lesson told of the long strain on the Tuesday of that week. We are still at the Tuesday. Try to get the class into sympathy with the sternness of a love which had been so contemptuously rejected.

§ 1. *Marriage of the King's Son*

Still that terrible Tuesday in the Temple, with its long strain of teaching and of conflict. Picture the fierce clerics round Him, trying to entrap Him by smart questions, or to lower in some way His credit with the multitude. Picture the crowd in the Temple listening with interest and sympathy as He quietly parried these attacks of the priests, and solemnly and steadily administered blow after blow to them in that public place, where they had always been supreme. Like a Master coming back to take account of His caretakers, He scourges them with rebuke after rebuke. Last Lesson He had spoken the parable of the Two Sons, and of the Wicked Husbandmen. Tell me them briefly, and recollect their sharp lesson, and the warning as to what God would do to these men. Were the priests and Pharisees pleased? What did they try to do? Why did they not? (xxi. 45, 46.)

Therefore He spoke the next parable. As he looked in their faces, and saw the look of murderous hate, and the attempt to seize Him foiled by their fear of the mob, He turns on them with another stinging rebuke. And again in the form of a story. He had a wonderful power of teaching by stories. What a delightful Sunday School Teacher the Lord would have been!

Tell me the story carefully, omitting none of the details. Is it like the story of Wicked Husbandmen? What is the main teaching of both? The guilt of the Jewish leaders in rejecting the Son of God. What did the husbandmen do to the son? What did the rejectors in this parable do? And in both it is clearly taught that when God in His great love came down to earth to save and bless men, and lift them up to live the "Beautiful Life" on earth, that He will be angry if they turn away from Him, and refuse to receive Him.

§ 2. Its Lesson for the Jews

Now come to details. We think first of its lesson for

the Jews. Who is the King? The Son? What is meant by feast? (*v.* 2.) The Kingdom of Heaven. You remember the whole teaching of St. Matthew is about this beautiful Kingdom of Heaven, which the Lord was founding to make all men's lives happy, and holy, and beautiful (Lesson III). Our Lord says it is as happy as a feast. The prophets, looking forward to it, used to say the same (Isaiah xxv. 6; lxv. 13). In parable of the Husbandmen it is spoken of as duty and service. That is also true. But our Lord teaches that that duty and service is the happiest work any boy or girl can do: "As happy as a feast," He says.

How many sets of invitations given to the Jews? Two? More, I think. Examine passage carefully, and see if you can find three (*v.* 3). Yes; them that *were bidden* already. Who do you think are meant by the servants? Probably (1) prophets; (2) John the Baptist and the Twelve in first mission (Matthew x.); (3) the Apostles and teachers from the Resurrection to destruction of Jerusalem. How were the first and second invitations received? Was it not kind of God to send a third invitation, even after the Jews had crucified Jesus? How were the third messengers received? How was that statement fulfilled? (Acts v. 40; xiv. 5-19; xvi. 23; vii. 58; xii. 2, etc.)

How did the King feel about it? Do you wonder He should? And the more angry because He had been so intensely in earnest to get them to come and be happy. If a man ask another to dinner, as a mere matter of form, without caring whether he came or not, he would not be angry at refusal; but if he were very eager to get him he would feel it much more. With God, the acceptance or rejection of His invitation was a most serious matter. He was greatly in earnest about it. And so, when the Jews only mocked at it, and crucified the Lord, and after that still refused and persecuted, God was angry with them, and inflicted a terrible punishment. How described in parable? (*v.* 7.) What really happened? Jerusalem destroyed utterly by the Roman armies. But it is said the King sent *His* armies. How? God uses as His instruments men who never thought of being such. (Isaiah x. 5: "O Assyrian, the rod of *mine* anger;" Ezekiel xvi. 41; Jeremiah xxii. 7, etc.) When a nation is destroyed by the armies of another nation, it may often be because it was God's will for some reason. Therefore the Roman armies here might be called "God's armies."

Did the king's feast, therefore, remain without guests? How was it filled up? (*vv.* 8-10.) Meaning? Yes. Jewish Church finally destroyed at the destruction of Jerusalem, and the Gentiles from all nations were invited out of all nations into God's Church. That is what gives us our chance to-day.

§ 3. Its Lessons for Us

After Jewish Church rejected, God's *fourth* set of invitations were sent out. To whom? By whom? And we are the peoples now all over the world to whom this invitation comes. What is the lesson for us? Not to refuse it. We see how terribly God was troubled by the Jews' refusal. "They made light of it." Do any Gentiles do so now? Do any boys and girls? "They went, one to his farm, and another to his merchandise," and neglected

God. Do any Gentiles do so? Country people thinking of their farms, and townspeople of their merchandise, and neglecting God's invitation to love and follow Him. The Lord has looked down on many nations since, and on many Sunday schools, and He has had to bear the pain of seeing this happen. I hope it will not be so here.

§ 4. *The Wedding Garment*

From *vv.* 11-14 is a sort of little extra parable added on which specially affects us. What is it about? It was a warning for the people who were listening. They heard that everybody could go into the Kingdom; that bad and good were invited in (*v.* 10). Does God, then, not care whether we are bad or good? What then? Why does He invite the bad? That they may become good. Now, some of the people might think that they could come into Christ's Kingdom, and yet remain bad and careless. Could they?

So He tells of King coming in to inspect the guests. When? Day of Judgment. What did He find? Meaning of wedding garment? Righteousness, nobleness of character, which the power of God's Holy Spirit creates in us. Had the man in parable any excuse? No. Speechless. Could the man say in excuse, "I could not get garment"? No, because the King provided them. Can we say, "Could not get righteousness and nobleness"? Why not? Yes. King provides them for all who want. "Blessed are they who hunger and thirst after righteousness, for they shall be filled." God is looking down on this school to-day.

All called into His Kingdom. Shall He find by-and-by that any of us is without the wedding garment of the righteous, unselfish, Christ-like life? God forbid.

§ 5. *Laying Traps for Him Again*

Did this solemn warning do the Pharisees any good? What did they do? (*v.* 15.) Tell me of three attempts to lay traps for Him, and by whom? His answers to each? So you see their clever plots did not succeed. But does it not show an awful spirit of wickedness, that, instead of repenting and asking His forgiveness, they should only become more spiteful and hostile? So it went on till they killed Him.

Notice in the second question the cause of many errors about God—not knowing the Scriptures. Notice in the third that He divides up the Law of God as the Church Catechism does. According to the Rabbis, there were 600 precepts of the Law, and many of their silly disputes were as to which was the greater. They thought to drag the Lord into these disputes. What a grand, lofty, simple answer! The whole Law is in these two—Love to God; Love to man.

ANGER AND PITY

St. Matthew XXIII.

Remind the class that we are still in the Week of the Passion, and still at that eventful Tuesday. Recapitulate briefly last Lesson. Solemn warning of the Lord. The response of His enemies to that warning, not repentance, but further attempts to lay traps for Him. He is now about to leave the Temple for ever. "Your house," said He, "is left unto you desolate;" and before He goes He must pronounce, sternly and sorrowfully, His terrible woes upon their hypocrisy and wrong-doing. Divide the chapter into two sections (*vv.* 1-12, and *v.* 12 to end). During the first the Pharisees and priests had evidently gone away, probably to carry out their evil designs; then at *v.* 13 picture them as suddenly returning and being received and overwhelmed with the indignant outburst of the eight woes.

§ 1. *The Anger of Christ*

Still this eventful Tuesday. I suppose it is now late in the afternoon. The Lord must be getting very tired with the long strain on His nerves. And still His enemies are watching to entrap Him. No dread about His warnings, no sorrow about His keen disappointment. He has gone against them. He has publicly rebuked them. He has turned all their clever questions back upon themselves. And, therefore, they hate Him with a deadly hatred. They have resolved that He must die if they can in any way manage it. And He has resolved so, too. He is now about to leave these Temple courts for ever. But first He must openly pronounce His terrible woes on their hypocrisy and wickedness. Don't you think that will make them hate Him more? Yes; but what matter, since He is resolved to die? And perhaps it will startle them, or startle the people, and make them think about their sin.

I want to impress on you that our Lord could be very angry. Some people don't understand that. They think of Him as always very soft and gentle. I fear they almost think of Him as weak. Don't you think that one who is always soft and gentle would be weak? For if the rich ill-treat the poor, and the crafty cheat the simple; if a big, strong bully ill-use a little girl, what would you think of the man who could not feel anger and indignation? He would surely be weak, and not worthy of high respect. Therefore, anger must exist in the character of Christ. Anger must exist in us, too. But anger for what? For own little vexations? No. Anger for the sake of the helpless, for the sake of righteousness, for the sake of God.

Who were the helpless that our Lord was angry for? The poor, ignorant crowds, "like sheep without a shepherd." Who were injuring them? Their clergy and teachers. Show me in what way chiefly? (*v.* 13.) God had given these men cleverness, and learning, and high position as leaders of His people, and therefore their sin was the more terrible. And therefore His indignation the stronger. And with all the indignation there was pity even for these wicked men. The indignation is there; but what most strikes us is the deep compassion in the warnings that the end of those evil tempers must be woe and ruin to them and to their country.

§ 2. *The People and Their Clergy*

To whom is He speaking in *v.* 1? The priests and Pharisees had probably gone away, shamed and crestfallen, to complete their wicked plots against Him. And I think the people must have been puzzled at the thought, "How are we to be guided since our teachers are so bad?" What does He direct? They are your appointed teachers. Do whatever they tell you. He meant: whatever they tell you *out of the Bible,* not their little quibbles and false interpretation of it. How do I know? (See *ch.* xv. 3-6; xvi. 6, 11, 12, etc.) It is a wonderful thing that while they so constantly corrupted the meaning of the Bible, they are never anywhere accused of corrupting or meddling with the words of it. They guarded it scrupulously, almost superstitiously. To their care we owe much for the preservation of the Bible. So, I think He meant, "These are your appointed clergy—guardians of God's Holy Word. Whatever they teach out of it, do. But do not copy their deeds. They say, and do not."

What conduct of theirs does He blame? *Binding on men's shoulders*, i.e., the little minute regulations and vexatious observances which they call religion. The poor foolish people thought these things were religion, and tried hard to do them; but their clergy never troubled to do them themselves. *Do deeds to be seen of men.* Our Lord does not like that in anybody. What does He say of it in Sermon on the Mount? (*ch.* vi. 1, 2.) But it was the common habit of these Pharisees. What does St. John say of them? "They loved the praise of men more than the praise of God" (John xii. 43). *Make broad their phylacteries,* i.e., make broad the coloured texts of Scripture on their robes, to draw attention to their extraordinary piety. Even if they *had* been pious, would God like this? But why was it worse in their case? It was hypocrisy. *They love the chief place*, etc., i.e., haughty, proud, despising others, and wanting to be put above everybody. What motto of His Kingdom of God does He repeat here to contrast Christian humility, which He loves, with the pride and vanity of the Pharisees? (*vv.* 11, 12.) Where said before? (*ch.* xx. 26, 27.)

§ 3. *The Eight Woes*

All this time He is talking quietly to the people; but now in a moment (at *v.* 13) His whole tone changes. Why, do you think? I think just at this moment the lawyers and Pharisees came back to listen. And the people started, as they saw in a moment the new stern look in His eyes, and heard His voice ring out over the whole crowded court, "Woe unto you, ye hypocrites!

Woe unto you, ye blind guides!" By this time they must have been quite cowed and frightened before Him. They never thought the gentle young prophet could say such terrible words. We had better see against what were these terrible woes directed.

The first woes were against their *teaching*, and the last against their *characters*.

Look at some of them. What is the first? (*v.* 13.) How? They prevented men from accepting Christ, and so entering His "Kingdom of Heaven" by their opposition and their false teaching about Scripture. Many a time the people were ready to follow Christ, and receive Him as Messiah. If the Pharisees would accept Him, all would be well. But they threw the whole weight of their authority against Him, and brought all their prejudices, and hatred, and slander to bear on him. So the poor simple people missed this great blessing. If these men had honestly believed what they said, would He have blamed them, even though it was against Himself? No, I am sure He would not. But they were moved only by spite and prejudice.

V. 15. "To make one proselyte." Meaning? Is it not right to make a proselyte? Since Jews believed they had the right religion, were they not right in doing so? Would we not be right in the case of Roman Catholics or Protestants of other religious bodies? Yes, if it was love for their souls, and desire to teach them truer teaching that would be more helpful in their lives, or make them more helpful to others. But with these Jews it was not love of souls, nor desire for God's glory. It was pride and vanity and covetousness and party spirit. They wanted just to win men over to their side, and to boast of it. A great many historians and ancient authors give us sad accounts of their proselytizing. So in our case. If Protestants want to proselytize from Roman Catholics in order to be proud of it, and boast of their converts—or if they offer inducements of money, or work, or clothes to get them to change their beliefs—it is a sin and would be condemned by our Lord and would probably do harm to the converts, and make them worse than before.

V. 16. Then comes their absurd teaching about oaths, which would upset all honesty. Of course, if a man solemnly promised at all to do a thing, he would, in God's sight, be bound without any oath. In fact, the Lord forbade oaths altogether. But the scribes and Pharisees taught their silly distinctions. If a man swear by a word that has not some letter of God's name in it, it is not binding. If a man swear by the Temple, it is not binding; but if by the gold of the Temple, it is; and so on. So that the people would have their ideas of right and wrong quite confused by their teachers.

V. 23. But their conduct was worse still than their teaching. Tithe, anise and cumin—i.e., they were most particular in giving to the Temple the tenth even of the potherbs in the garden. Quite right so far. What was wrong, then? Ah yes. They set such great store on these petty trifles, and left undone the important matters—judgment, mercy, faithfulness. Did not mind being unjust, unmerciful, unfaithful, so long as the little petty things, like the tithe of potherbs in the garden were all right. They, as the old proverb says, "strain at the gnat and swallow the camel." I fear some are like them still. Very particular about little outward observances of religion, and often bitter, and gloomy, and unfair, and unkind at home.

V. 25. Cup and platter—i.e. woe against mere external and ceremonial purification. Hands washed often. Dress, food, vessels, everything, kept pure from any ceremonial defilement. All this is but to teach the duty of having a pure heart. But the pure heart itself they never think of.

V. 27. What does He mean by "whited sepulchres?" Travellers still tell us of the whitewashed tombs in Palestine. Every year they were newly whitewashed. "Ye are like those tombs," said the Lord, "white and pure in outward appearance: inwardly full of rottenness." Hypocrisy is especially hateful to Him. Bad enough to be wicked; but to be wicked and pretend to be a saint is far worse.

Sterner and more solemn grew His words as He went on. I think He saw the look of hate deepening in their eyes. He saw the fixed determination to kill Him. So He cries out, "Fill up, then, the measure of your fathers' cruelty. They killed the prophets. You will kill every good man whom God sends to you. Ye serpents, ye vipers, how shall ye escape the judgment of hell!" They were terrible words. They show the terrible anger of God against hypocrisy and spiteful, unrelenting hatred. And they show it the more coming from the lips of Him who was so loving to the little children. It must have been a great sin that forced such words from Him. He shows the greatness of their sin by telling what they will do to His disciples after they have killed Himself. What? Tell me any instance of its fulfilment?

§ 4. The Wail of Rejected Love

The last verses of the chapter prove that His sorrow and pity were even deeper than His anger. In the midst of His stern words His voice suddenly breaks, as He thinks of all His hopes, and efforts, and longings to save that Jewish race, and how all had been foiled and rejected. Such a simple, homely figure, and yet how full of beautiful meaning! A hen, when the hawk soars up into the sky, in terrible anxiety calling the little chickens to shelter. "And ye would not." "Ye would not." That is the sad complaint of Christ in the world still. I think of all the classes in the school—the figure fits so well for children—and the Lord crying over some of them to-day, "How often would I have gathered you. I would, but ye would not." Children, don't let it be so with you when you grow up. Don't disappoint the strong, patient love that is over you. If the silly chickens take no heed of the mother's call, they must surely be snapped up by the hawk. That is the greatest pain you can give the Lord Jesus. Don't give it. Cling to Him. Nestle close to Him. Pray to Him always—

> "Cover my defenceless head
> With the shadow of Thy wing."

LESSON XIX

HOW HE SETS US TO WAIT TILL HE COMES

St. Matthew XXIV. 1-4, and 36 to end, and XXV. to v. 14.

Remember, in last Lesson, the Lord's terrible denunciations, and His solemn and sorrowful farewell to the temple and the people. He had made His final effort, His final appeal. Now He could do no more to ward off their fate. The evil must come.

Probably the disciples had no conception of the great and solemn thoughts which filled His heart. How do you know? So proud of their beautiful temple; wanted Him to admire it. How sorrowfully He answers to their innocent boasting. What? Must have completely startled them for the moment. They cannot get it out of their heads; and as He sits down to rest on His way back to Bethany, they come to ask Him—what?

His answer is a series of prophecies, difficult to explain to children. They begin with the destruction of Jerusalem, and gradually merge into the great Second Advent. It is not easy to apportion exactly the

163

separate parts of the prophecy; but the closing part, which we take for this Lesson, is perfectly clear. Their question is—"Tell us when," etc. (*v.* 3). And His answer in *vv.* 36-51. What is it? Briefly this: No one knows the time. Therefore, the only way to be prepared is to be always ready. What does He say of the faithful and unfaithful servant? Then, in *ch.* xxv., He gives two wonderful pictures of that coming. What do we call the two parables? We take the first to-day, and the other next Lesson.

§ 1. The Waiting Virgins

First tell me the story. Yes. Marriages in the East then and now celebrated at night. The bridegroom, accompanied by his friends, "the children of the bridechamber," "the friends of the bridegroom" (Matthew ix. 15; John iii. 29; Judges xiv. 11), went to bride's house, and led her with great rejoicing to his own home. She was accompanied from her father's house by her youthful friends and companions (Psalm xlv. 15), whilst others of these, the "virgins" of the parable, met the procession on the way, and entered with the rest into the hall of feasting.[3]

It is very like what happens to-day. Here is an account by a recent traveller of a marriage which he saw in India: "The bridegroom came from a distance, and the bride lived at Serampore, to which place the bridegroom was to come by water. After waiting two or three hours, at length, near midnight, it was announced, as if in the very

[3] Trench on Parables.

words of Scripture: 'Behold the bridegroom cometh; go ye out to meet him.' All the persons employed now lighted their lamps, and ran with them in their hands to fill up their stations in the procession. Some of them had lost their lights, and were unprepared; but it was then too late to seek them, and the cavalcade moved forward to the house of the bride, at which place the company entered a large and splendidly illuminated area before the house, covered with an awning, where a great multitude of friends, dressed in their best apparel, were seated upon mats. The bridegroom was carried in the arms of a friend, and placed upon a superb seat in the midst of the company, where he sat a short time, and then went into the house, the door of which was immediately shut, and guarded by sepoys. I and others expostulated with the doorkeepers, but in vain. Never was I so struck with our Lord's beautiful parable as at this moment: 'And the door was shut.'"

§ 2. Who Are the Wise and Foolish Virgins?

Now, remember that the purpose of the parable is to enforce the precept, "Be ye always ready." What are the two considerations to keep them always ready? (1) "Ye know that the Second Coming shall be; (2) but ye do not know *when* it shall be." Show me that both are necessary in order to keep people watchful.

Now for the meaning of the parable. Who is the Bridegroom? Who are meant by wise and foolish virgins? Good and bad people, you say! Do you all think that is quite correct? Why not? Notice first that they all regard themselves as friends of the Bridegroom. Bad, wicked people would not do that. I don't believe He is thinking of the openly irreligious people at all. It is a picture of professedly Christian people, who go regularly to church, and probably say their prayers, and sometimes read their Bibles, and who are not openly showing any disloyalty to Christ. They all seem, to themselves and to others, to be Christ's friends and followers. They all hope to go in with Him to the marriage supper of the Lamb.

Who, then, are the wise and foolish virgins? Better see first what is the difference between them. One set carried a supply of oil for the lamp; the other did not. Therefore we have to ask further, what is meant by (1) the light, (2) the oil. For the first we see our Lord's use of the word "light" elsewhere, e.g., "Let your light so shine before men," etc. The light evidently means the *visible side* of Christian character, manifested in acts of righteousness. Therefore the oil should mean the *inward supply* which feeds that light, or, in other words, the grace of God's Holy Spirit.

Now you can tell me who are the foolish virgins. Who? Not Christless, profane, ungodly people. They are people whose light was once burning, who had some inward grace of the Holy Spirit in their hearts; but it got used up, and they did not renew it; those not watchful of their spiritual life, negligent in prayer, slothful in effort, whose religious life is daily dwindling away till it vanishes altogether.

Who are the wise virgins? Those who know that

religion means more than religious emotions and feelings, who are earnest, through daily prayer and Bible-reading and sacrament, to nourish with the Divine oil the light of their good life.

§ 3. Both the Oil and the Light Needed

Oliver Cromwell on his death-bed asked his chaplain, "If a man be once in the grace of God, can he ever fall away from it?" "No," said the chaplain. "Then," said the dying man, "it must be right with me, for I know I was once in the grace of God." What should this parable have taught to Cromwell? That for men to be in the grace of God is not everything.

We are brought into God's grace at our Baptism. Many who fall away are brought back into it at conversion. But that is not enough. They are but in the condition of the ten virgins starting out. They are but in the beginning of the life-road. Their lamps are only just lighted. They have yet to be tested whether they will keep in the life-road, whether they will keep up the supply of the oil in their lamps. Whose fault if they do not? God's? No. God's grace is at their disposal all through life. But it must be sought. How? Yes. And men may neglect prayer and Holy Communion and reading of the Bible, and all the means of grace. If so, will the light keep burning till the Master come? This is a terrible warning, that the light of a righteous life cannot be kept on without taking care of the supply of oil.

But, on the other hand, the oil without being used

for light will not do either. The oil is of no use except to produce light. No man can store up God's grace *for himself*. He must use it. The Bible-reading and prayer and sacraments will cease to bring help if the grace is not being used to do righteous deeds. The supply of oil will fail utterly if it is not being used in the good deeds of a righteous life. We want both the light and the supply of oil to be ready to meet the Bridegroom.

§ 4. While They Slumbered

Was it wrong? I don't think so. For it is said of both wise and foolish alike—with no word of blame. In the early Church they expected Christ's return every day. "He may come this morning, this evening, any moment." But, as "the Bridegroom tarried," as years and centuries rolled on, the eagerness naturally calmed down, the expectation grew less intense, till now, after nineteen hundred years, we have grown quiet, and calm, and unexcited. We know, as the early Christians did, that He may come any day; but we cannot help taking it more quietly. It is only natural.

And the merciful lesson of the parable seems to be, that God wants not so much that we should be feverishly watching, but that we should be quietly ready. True, the more we love Him, the more we shall look forward; but the important thing is that we should so live that, whenever He comes, He should find us ready. Does that mean always in church, at prayer, etc.? No. But doing all our ordinary work as in His presence. Story of Massachusetts senator in time of excitement about

Second Advent. The hall grew suddenly dark at midday. Men sprang up in terror. It is the Lord's coming! "Well," said the old senator, "what if it is! How better can our Lord find us engaged than doing our duty? Bring in the lights, and proceed with the business."

HOW HE SETS US OUR WORK TILL HE COMES

St. Matthew XXV. 14 to end.

Remind of Parable of Ten Virgins in last Lesson. To-day companion parable. Difference between them, that while the former emphasizes keeping the *heart* with all diligence, this has to do with putting that diligence into *work*. That tells of duty of right state of heart while you wait. This tells of duty of *working* while you wait. During the great waiting-time between the going away of our Lord and His return, He has given "to every man his work."

§ 1. Setting the Work

First, tell me the story carefully only up to the time that the man "went on his journey." Notice margin of Revised Version: "bond-servants" = "slaves." Not quite our idea of slaves' work. But would be understood then. I read once a Russian story telling of like conditions. Slaves, if artizans, found work, and paid the master so many roubles a year; if dealers or pedlars, took money, and made profit with it for him. Who are meant by "the man" and the "servants"? What sums did this man give? For what purpose? For *trading*, that they might make profit to enrich their master.

What is meant by talents?[4] Gifts, endowments, advantages, opportunities given by God to His servants. Have boys and girls got any? Tell me what they are. For this whole story has reference to you. What is meant by the dissimilar amounts? Yes, that God does not start all men equally with brains, or position, or wealth, or opportunity, or even with equal help of His grace. One boy is cleverer, or richer, or in better position, or with more religious influences around him than another. Five talents, or two, or one. Notice that Christ recognises no case of having *no* talent. Every one of you here has something given him by God. (Convince of this before you go on.)

All the gifts given for what? For *trading*, to enrich the master. Meaning? That our talents, and gifts, and opportunities are not merely for ourselves. God gives them as a means of making profit for Him. What profit does He want? Gains for Himself? Surely not. But God has a tremendous work to do for this poor world to make it happier, and holier, and nobler in every way; and He will not do it except through His servants. If they will not work, all must fail. He has appointed no

---

[4]To be perfectly accurate, the natural abilities are not exactly what is meant here. These are rather the "several ability," according to which were given the talents of position, and opportunities, measure of grace, etc. But with children this is too fine a distinction. It would only puzzle them. All gifts and endowments may be included.

other way. Therefore are our gifts given. No boy, or girl, or man, or Church, or nation ever received any gift or endowment for himself alone; but that he might with it help others, and make life better and nobler.

Now be clear about this. God has set "to every man his work." What do you think of the person who, at close of life, thinks all must be right with him, "because," he says, "I have never done much harm to anybody." Is that enough? Why not? Why, of course, because God has sent him into the world, not merely to keep from doing harm, but to do work. Fancy a builder coming to his men, and finding them all idle, and boasting that they had done no harm! How silly it would seem! What is the work set you? At present to be kindly and unselfish, to be earnest in religion, to do your school-work and other work given you, and so develop your talents for bigger work hereafter; by-and-by to do your part for God, to help to make life better and happier for men.

§ 2. How Talents Increase and Decrease

Now go on with story. Tell me of the master's return, and the trading servants handing in their accounts. What is meant by the talents increasing to two talents, and five talents more? Would they have increased if left unused? Did any of the servants try this? How were they increased? By using. So with all God's gifts. *He that useth increaseth. He that useth not shall lose.* Repeat this three times over for me, all of you. Did you ever see this happen? Blacksmith's great muscle in arm. Why greater than yours? Musician's skill on piano. Savage's keen eye in the forest. The blind man's keen sense of touch, that can distinguish one man from another by touching the clothes. Why all these powers greater than those of others? Because of using constantly. And so with spiritual life. Why is it easier for an old man to love and obey God after doing so earnestly for sixty years of his life? The great Law of Gain in all life—*He that useth increaseth.*

There is also corresponding Law of Loss. Illustrate. We saw gain in blacksmith's arm. Now, suppose instead of using his arm, he had when a boy tied it up to his side for life? It would shrivel up, muscle would waste away. Compare eye of savage in forest with eye of the mole under the ground. The mole is blind. Why? Because never used eyes for generations and generations. God's great law is, "If you don't use, you shall lose." Mammoth caves of Kentucky—great caves, pitch-dark, full of water. Travellers tell us most interesting stories of them. The fish and frogs are quite blind. They have eyes, but quite dead and sightless. Why? Never use them. So if boy's mind never exercised with thought or with lessons, it would become stupid, and finally idiotic. Same of soul's life. If a man never obeys conscience, never thinks of God, never prays, his conscience will get dulled; he will find it more and more difficult to think of God or to pray. Why? State the Law of Loss for me. *He that useth not shall lose.* That is the explanation of many a dead, careless life to-day. It is a terrible warning.

§ 3. The Master Who Loves To Praise People

Note, in *v. 19, a long time.* Perhaps a hint that the Second Coming not so near as they thought. What is meant by the master coming back to take account of his servants? When? At his second coming. Tell me accurately the *first* words of the *three* servants? (*vv.* 20, 22, 24.) That is, the two first began with glad, grateful acknowledgment that it was God who had given them all they had to begin with. They think of God as the kind giver. The other thinks only of God as the strict, stern demander. That makes a great difference in one's work.

Had the two good servants gained same sum? Yet they got same praise. Why? If each had gained two talents, would praise have been equal? Why not? Does God expect same work from all? What then? Each to be faithful *according to his ability.* Not *quantity* of the work so important as the *quality* and *motive.* So God is very fair and loving to the stupid, and to the poor struggler who finds it hard to do right. "Only be faithful," He says. What is His praise? "Well done, *successful* servant? Or *brilliant* servant?" No, but—faithful.

And see in this parable how God loves to praise us. Of course, the work of these men was imperfect. Fault-finders could easily pick holes in it. But not so God. Hear that hearty "well done!" The generous, hearty praise of Him who loves to praise, and hates to find fault. Ah! young people, it is nice to have a Master such as that.

§ 4. *The Reward for Service Is Higher Service*

A very interesting question. When a man has developed his talents, and abilities, and spiritual life given to him, what is God's reward? Is it that the men and women should be idlers, and "go out on pension," as it were? Is it that the boys and girls should cease the active life of work, and sit down in a big church in heaven for all eternity? Honestly, should you like that? Well, what is the reward for work? (*vv.* 21, 23.) The reward is more, and grander, and higher work. Just as here, when a man has done well in a small position, he gets a bigger position, where he can do greater and more useful work. All who have done useful work for God below, will be rewarded by doing nobler and higher, unselfish work for all eternity above. We cannot tell what endless possibilities of service God has for us.

Boys and girls, full of health and eagerness, could not rest without doing things; and God has eternal doing for them. Heaven is our eternal service, but heaven is not an eternal church service. Nay, there is no church at all in heaven (Revelations xxi. 22), for all life there is so full of God, and of joyous, unselfish work for others in His presence, that we shall not need to come at special times, to church to remind ourselves about Him. So live the true, high life here, and it will be true of you what was said of another faithful servant of God at death:—

"We doubt not that for one so true,
There must be other nobler work to do."

That is the "joy of the Lord," into which we shall enter, the joy of unselfish service in joyous, eternal youth for ever.

§ 5. The Man Who Would Not Use His Talent

Terrible warning. Why was this man cast out? Not for doing something terribly wicked, but for leaving undone all that he had been sent into the world to do. What excuse had he? Was afraid. The others had pleasant thoughts of God as a *giving* God. He had only hard thoughts of Him as a *demanding* God, hard to satisfy, who would make no allowances. Some people really have this feeling about God. But most of those who thus fail only use this as an excuse for their slothfulness. They act as if they had no work and no talents from God. They see wrong-doing amongst their comrades, and never object to it. They see efforts after right, and never try to help them. It is a terrible warning that it is not merely open opposition to God that destroys men, but also drifting through life and neglecting to use God's gifts for God's work.

What does the master say he might have done if he had not the courage of trading? Put it in bank. Not quite sure of meaning. Bank is where they take in a number of small, insignificant sums, and invest them in some big undertaking. Perhaps the Lord meant that if you could not do any big work yourself, you might join some society where there were leaders able to direct, and which would use your little efforts with those of others for some great undertaking—e.g., Missionary

Society, to bring together the prayers, and efforts, and contributions of many insignificant individuals to do a great work for missions; or the Temperance Society, or any other organization which tries to rouse public opinion for social reform, bringing together separate individuals who separately would have no weight. Perhaps the Lord meant something like that.

What was the punishment? Take away his talent. Why? Not used. Meaning? God is always doing that. Remember our illustrations earlier. God allows no man to keep any talent, or power, or spiritual grace without using it. The law of God is that it shall die out and be lost. And, worst of all, the man was cast out of God's presence into the outer darkness, instead of having the hearty, generous "Well done! Enter into the joy of thy Lord."

FOUR SCENES BEFORE THE END

St. Matthew XXVI. to v. 31.

Scene I

The supper at Bethany (*vv.* 6-14). Why do I put this first? Read John xii. 1-6. Six days before. Therefore, though St. Matthew tells it here, owing to its connection with Judas, it was really on the Saturday night before Palm Sunday. Remainder of events in this chapter were during Holy Week, i.e., just before Crucifixion. Simon the Leper, probably Martha's husband, or the father of the whole Bethany family. Not improbable that the healing of him was Christ's first introduction to the family. Possibly this banquet was in rejoicing about resurrection of Lazarus. Was ever a stranger banquet—a man who had lain dead in the grave four days sitting at table with One who was God in human form! Surely there must have been deep emotion in all their hearts!

Deeper and intenser that emotion grew as Mary

came in. There was a very close friendship between these Bethany sisters and the Lord. It was rest to Him to sit and talk with them; and I am sure that what He had repeatedly told His disciples of late, He had confided to them, too—that He was to die this Passover. So you can picture Mary, with her deep devotion to Him, and her intense gratitude about Lazarus, now coming to learn that He to whom she owed everything was about to be put to death within a week, and you will understand the emotion which filled her heart, and prompted her to pour out of her costliest treasures for Him. Nothing that she could give would be sufficient to express her feelings. Three hundred pence! it seemed but the most paltry trifle. Would that it were a thousand times as much, that it might better express her love! Don't you think the Lord, Who knew her heart, would be touched by such love? There was not too much of love round Him that week in Jerusalem.

But everybody else did not feel as He did. Tell me of the grumbling. Who began it? (St. John xii.) Why? Were they right? Would it not be better to give it to poor? What did the Lord say? Same thing still said when large sum given for beautiful church. Is it right to neglect orphans and poor for this? No; but those who thus give really for sake of God's glory always give well to the poor also. Not deprive the poor, but deprive themselves, to give to God. And very often the grumblers give little to either. It entirely depends on the motive. And Christ, Who saw the motive, accepted it lovingly, and promised that her beautiful deed should be a memorial for ever. He thought that three hundred pence was of little importance when weighed against that deep, strong, passionate devotion to Him.

Scene II

Tuesday night. Caiaphas' house near the Temple. Conspirators gathering in one by one out of the moonlight. Pharisee, Sadducee, Herodian, Priest and Scribe, Annas and Caiaphas, bigots and atheists, all banded together in conspiracy against the young Teacher, Who had dared everything for the truth. How fiercely they hated Him! Such men as they could never forgive Him. Not merely that they thought He was endangering the political existence of the nation. There was personal hatred besides. They had been defeated and shamed in open encounter in the presence of the people. They had been shown up as ignorant and hypocritical. This uneducated young Rabbi from the country had turned on them as a master would turn on a crouching slave, and lashed them with these terrible, scathing woes, that they, or the people who heard them, could never forget. He had been so gentle up to this time that they never dreamed that He could turn on them like that. Never could they forgive it. Die he must.

But when? Not on the feast day. Wait till the people dispersed, and only a few disciples with him. It must be soon, but not on the Passover. Ah! but it must be on the Passover. Why? (*v.* 2.) Probably at that moment He was telling His disciples, "Ye know that after two days is the Feast of the Passover, and the Son of Man must be betrayed," etc. He had quite settled that during the

Passover, when they commemorated the slaying of the Paschal lamb in Egypt, must be slain the great Paschal Lamb, of whom this was but a type and shadow.

And now comes a marvellous overruling of evil to bring about God's purpose. Even while they were discussing it, something happened to make them do it at Passover. What? A knock at the door; a message brought in: "A disciple of Jesus the Nazarene is outside." Just what they wanted. "I will betray Him unto you in the absence of the multitude. I know His secret places of prayer—haunts at Gethsemane and elsewhere. What will ye give me?" What did they give? Yes—seems very little—perhaps only an instalment; perhaps with the Jewish bargaining spirit, they beat down his price by saying that they could easily get Him without any guide a few days later. At any rate, the bargain was made, the blood-money paid over, and the Holy and Just One was sold, just when He was out alone at Bethany praying for the poor sinful world that He had come to redeem.

Scene III

Jesus alone in His little room at Bethany, or out on the lonely hillside, preparing for the end. He seems to have spent all the Wednesday and Thursday in deep seclusion, preparing, we may believe, for the terrible struggle of Gethsemane and Calvary. We may feel sure that, as on that other night, a crisis in His life, "He continued all night in prayer to God."

Don't miss the contrast. Look at the two pictures. In the one picture the chamber of conspirators—scribes, and priests, and Pharisees; the gentry and the clergy, and leaders of the people, with wealth and comfort, and earthly prosperity, and power to destroy the man whom they hated. In the other picture, a hard-handed young Carpenter, poor, and despised, and hated, and about to be to-morrow execrated by the mob, and murdered by the law; with nothing to comfort Him but the calm sense of right and duty, and the deep consciousness of the Father's presence and approval. Which would you rather be? Though all the comfort and wealth on the one side, and all the discomfort and poverty on the other? Yes. Learn thus in what consists the true value and nobleness of life. For it was not because He was divine that He could endure so nobly. It is the grace given to every true heart who dares everything for the right.

Scene IV

The Last Supper. The Lord and the Twelve sitting, or rather reclining, at the Passover. Explain the way of reclining round the table. It is their last night together, and they are saddened and troubled. And He, too, is burdened in heart. Think of the sorrow to Him who knew all things. Knew that these twelve whom He had chosen to be His closest friends would all fail Him— Peter deny—Judas betray—all the rest run away from the danger, and leave Him. How that great love was disappointed then. And *now* also. But he is thinking of their sorrow, not of His own. St. John tells us how He comforted them (St. John xiv. 1). How like Him—never to think of Himself, but only of others.

Suddenly a startling announcement: "One of you shall betray Me." Did they suspect Judas? Or each other? (*v.* 22.) Wonderful humility and brotherliness. Each only mistrusted himself. Could it possibly be me? Surely none of us would do it! Judas, too, asks "Is it I?" He wants to see if the Lord is as unsuspicious as his brethren. And in a low voice unheard by the others, Jesus answers him (*v.* 25). Should not this have startled him into giving up his sin? Still more awful words just before (*v.* 24). Think of the awful fact, which is true of some to-day also.

Now wine-cup passed round. Bread and bitter herbs eaten. Now a pause. Something very solemn happening? (*vv.* 26-28.) He was now putting an end to Jewish Passover. It had pointed in type to Him through all the centuries. He was the Lamb who should be slain. And now the type was about to be accomplished and done with. Instead of it, He would make a new and different festival. He took plain bread and plain wine, and blessed them, and by His mighty power decreed that when this was done by His Church in the days to come, it should be a means of our receiving spiritual strength, receiving in some wonderful way His own self into our souls. What says Catechism? What is the outward part? Inward? Benefits of which we are partakers thereby? You can't understand all this mystery; but you can understand at least two reasons why people should be regular communicants, and why you should when admitted to it after Confirmation. The first we have mentioned, "The strengthening and refreshing of our souls," etc. Surely people should not miss that.

What is the second reason? This: "Do it always," He said, "in remembrance of Me." "Don't forget Me. Let this be always the reminder to you of My love, and of the lives I want you to live for Me." Imagine a dying mother saying to her children: "Do this or that in remembrance of me. Once every month put fresh flowers on my grave." What a shame if neglected! How it would disappoint and sadden her if she could know. But that is a common sin with careless Christians. Think of this when you see the Holy Table arranged for Communion, and let it remind you of that night in upper room, and of the many who, by their neglect, disappoint and sadden the Lord. Say, "Lord, help me not to sadden or disappoint Thee. Lord, when I am old enough to be allowed to Thy Holy Table, I will try to go regularly in remembrance of Thee."

LESSON XXII

GETHSEMANE AND THE MOCK TRIAL

St. Matthew XXVI. 31 to end.

We are now drawing near the end. We are in presence of an awful mystery—the Great Deliverer needing deliverance—the Comforter of humanity looking for comfort. Be very reverent and solemn. Make the children feel that they are on holy ground. Teacher should spend much time beforehand in meditating and praying about this Lesson, and trying to enter into the solemn spirit of it, that his subdued tone and manner may express his inmost feelings. It is necessary for teacher to decide which parts of this Lesson he will dwell most on. It is far too long to teach it all fully.

Recapitulate last Lesson. Last Supper over. His good-bye to them. Had told them of parting—tried to comfort them about the future.

§ 1. The Farewell Prayer

(Before reading the chapter teach this section.)

To fully understand and enter into any scene in the Gospels, it is necessary to put together all the accounts of it. For instance, in this Lesson. We thought last day about the sad farewell meeting in Upper Room, and the institution of the Last Supper. But the story did not leave the impression of a long night sitting, of long, loving, sorrowful conversation hour after hour, closing with an earnest prayer of the Lord for His poor disciples whom He was leaving.

Now read *v.* 30, and then the corresponding verse, John xviii. 1—"When Jesus had spoken these words." What words? You look back in St. John's account (*ch.* xiv., xv., xvi., xvii.), and a whole new light flashes on the scene. You see after the institution of the Holy Communion they did not go out at once. Four hours they sat on in sad communing together, as the Lord poured out His soul to them, and they saw how deep was His love, how touching His utter forgetfulness of self. Glance at these chapters. "Let not your hearts be troubled." "I will not leave you comfortless." "I will send the Comforter." "I will come again to receive you to Myself," etc. And they sit listening like men around a friend's death-bed. And then when it is time to go, there is the solemn hush of expectancy. They see by His face that He is about to pray. I think there must have been tears and sobbing as they heard that prayer, so full of its exquisite sympathy and self-forgetfulness. All for them and for the future Church. (Read a few verses of the prayer, John xvii.) He knew of the wretched morrow—the betrayal and denial, the judgment, the mockery, the spitting on, and scourging, the awful agony of the Cross. But no thought for that, only for the lonely little band that He was leaving, and the future that lay before His infant Church. He was always like that. Utterly unselfish, utterly self-sacrificing. He is like that still in heaven to-day.

§ 2. Gethsemane

Read here only *vv.* 30 to 46. "When they had sung a hymn," probably the *Hallel*, the usual Passover hymn comprising Psalms cxiii.-cxviii. Read a few verses of this hymn. Then out in the bright moonlight they go along the Olivet road. The strain on His heart growing more severe—the intense craving for solitude—for prayer—for the Father's presence. He must be alone in His favourite praying-place. Talk on the road. Peter's impulsive reply. Peter always impulsive—like us Irish people (see again *v.* 33)—big, generous, impulsive heart, always rushing at things, not calm and quiet. Very confident. Not safe to be too confident. Safer a few hours before when he distrusted himself, and said, "Lord, is it I?" Be afraid of unaided self. Be very confident in God.

Now approaching very solemn sight. Right on to lonely glades of Gethsemane. All left behind but three. Who? When with Him before? Why bring them? His human craving for friendship in great trouble.

Verse 37. "He *began* to be," etc., as if a sudden wave of emotion breaking over His soul like a huge breaker sweeping in suddenly from the sea. "Sore troubled," restless agitation, intense mental distress. He who had been so quiet and self-possessed just before is now seized in the pangs of an uncontrollable anguish. How terrible it must have been when He, so reserved usually about Himself, so unwilling to talk of His own pains or discomforts, has wrung from Him the unutterably pathetic cry, "My soul is exceeding sorrowful, even *unto death*," i.e., "I Who know the limits of human endurance, feel that I am touching the very borders of death—just a little more, and my life would give way." And then notice in His deep trouble how touchingly He reaches out for comfort and sympathy. "Keep near Me, you three. Tarry you here," etc. As they tarry He hurries past. He must be on His knees. He must flee to the Father's presence for comfort and help. What blessed thing for anyone to have such a love of prayer and of God. Good for us if we can gain for ourselves such a blessed shelter in trouble.

Now we behold awful sight. Agony of mind so intense that even He could not bear it. He Who was so brave and calm to bear everything. Listen to tortured cry: "O, My Father! if it be possible, remove this cup from Me." Meaning of "cup." (See Mark x. 38, 39). What was this cup? Was it only the fear of death? Was it only the denial, betrayal, contempt, and scorn, awful death upon Cross, with mocking crowds around? Surely not. Bad as all these were, He was too brave to fear them. Even some of His humble martyrs have borne death without fear. What was it? We do not know. Cannot understand. Deep mystery of God. We only know that it came in some way from the awful burden of the sins of the world. Read Isaiah liii. 4-6. "The Lord hath laid on Him the iniquity of us all." All we can see is that it was some awful, intolerable agony of soul that came on the pure, holy Saviour from bearing the horrible burden of the world's sin.

Was it easy for Him to bear it? No. He had laid aside His Divine power—had to bear it as a man. You and I find it hard to do painful things for sake of God and duty. Wonderful and comforting to think, He found it hard, too. Terribly hard. "If it be possible, let it pass from Me." How awful it must have been! Is it wrong to feel it hard to do one's duty? No. Duty is all the grander when you feel it hard, and yet do it. The Lord had to force His human will to obey the Divine will, just as we have to do. But He determined to do it, however hard. That was the grand thing. Therefore He can understand our struggles to do it. Can sympathize with and pity us, and rejoice with us when we conquer like Himself. If He had kept His power as God to help Him, would it be half so grand or so helpful to us? What does He say about getting His own will? (*v.* 39.) No matter how hard to do or bear, let that be always our prayer. When it comes to praying that, the struggle grows quieter. Like as with our Lord, there comes a great calm—the calm of victory—and "there appeared an angel from heaven strengthening Him." So with us, too.

How many times did He go to see if disciples were keeping watch with Him? Why? His heart yearned for their comfort and sympathy. And what did He find each time? Yes. They failed Him—miserably, shamefully. Was He very angry? No. Would you be, if some day in horrible misery you found sisters or mother quietly sleeping while you were suffering! "Much they care,"

189

you would say angrily. You would not trouble to make allowances or excuses for them. Not so Jesus Christ. See what He says (*v.* 41): "Ah!" He says, "the spirit is willing enough; it is only the flesh that is weak." He knew it was not that they did not care, but they were so dead-tired—severe nervous strain all that night—perhaps up previous night with Him as well. Is it not touching to see Him actually apologizing for them, making excuses for them, trying to look for the good in them, where others would only see the evil? Is it not comforting to us to think He is like that—like a father with bad son looking for any little trace of good in him, delighted to find it, making every allowance for him—looking for the good motive at bottom of mistaken action—looking for the sorrow and penitence in his heart, when others only see his faults and his sin. Thank God we have such a loving Master.

§ 3. The Mock Trial

Read *v.* 57 to end. Most astonishing sight in history. The Judge of Mankind at the judgment bar of men! The Saviour of Mankind about to be killed by those whom He came to save! Think what a mockery. His judges are the men who hated Him for rebuking their sin, the men who sent out spies to trap Him, the men who tried to kill Him. Was there likelihood of fair play? Could these men, with their spite and cant and hypocrisy and self-seeking, form any true judgment as to character of the loving, self-sacrificing Christ? No more than a bat could judge the sunshine. They called witnesses—for what? to find out the truth? (*v.* 59.) Determined that He must die. Little they thought that thus they were doing what He wanted. He, too, was determined that He should die.

Picture scene.—The palace of high priest probably thus—(1) First, the *porch*, with pillars and porter's lodge. (2) From this doors opened into the *court* (*v.* 66), a long apartment open in middle to the sky. (3) Beyond this, reached by steps, the *judgment room* where the trial took place. Get class to make mental picture of it, with the judges assembled, and the Lord before them, pale and tired, with strong cords binding His hands, and "beneath in the court" (*court*, not *palace*, *v.* 69) Peter and the servants warming themselves. It seems when all fled, Peter and John ashamed, and came back (John xviii. 15), but afar off (Mark xiv. 54). Doorkeeper knew John, and let them in. This is how we get the account of the trial. They saw it. Tell me about the false witnesses (*vv.* 59-61). Did the witnesses succeed? It seemed as if He would get off free. They could not condemn Him. Was high priest pleased to see it? (*v.* 62.) Could not sit still—so angry at his failure, and calm, dignified silence of prisoner. "Why don't you answer?" he cries. Could He have explained this story about Temple? But He knew it would be no use. They only wanted an excuse to condemn Him. Did He get fiercely angry? Did He ever in His life get fiercely angry? Yes (Mark x. 14); but it was for other's sake, never for His own. He could be fearfully angry at one who had led a little child astray; but He could be grandly patient and silent when they were cruelly ill-treating Himself. What a beautiful soul was His! He is trying to make us like that. Are *we* trying? At last the high priest gets an answer. Stung beyond endurance at the quiet silence of the Lord, he asks—what? No more silence now. Calmly, solemnly the answer comes: "I am." And what more? How grand, how God-like, the answer! What a mean, unjust trial! If He had said "No," they would say "an impostor." He said "Yes," and they cried what? Thus was He condemned to death. Then comes the horrible, brutal treatment. We almost shrink from reading it. Fancy those brutal creatures cuffing and boxing Him; spitting in His face; tying bandages across His eyes, to make Him guess who struck Him! Oh, how could they! And He was their God! their Saviour! Is it not horrible? Yet, is it not beautiful to see such noble suffering? And is it not very touching for us?

> "I bore all this for thee;
>   What canst thou bear for Me?"

§ 4. The Testing of Peter

But another trial going on in the courtyard. What? Peter being tried. Poor Peter—found it much easier to be religious and confident before the danger came (*v.* 33). We never know till tested. Ashamed of running away, he had come in now, and tried to seem at ease, sitting with servants at fire, but very frightened. Would they find out about Malchus's ear? Suddenly without preparation his testing begins. How? (*v.* 69.) Did you ever tell a lie when suddenly asked, and you had not time to decide? So Peter now. A sudden temptation like that is a good test of us. Cultivate habit of bold, transparent truth always, and then you will never be taken unawares. Then he tried to escape this girl; out into the porch, where the groups of people waited. But the girl followed him, and repeated charge. What happened? How did the third suspicion come? Galilean accent—country brogue. Peter now utterly terrified. What a horrible thing! (*v.* 74.)

So God's testing of Peter was over. Peter had shamefully failed. Oh, how could he! With the Master who loved him being persecuted to death, and all the world against Him, would it not be better to suffer anything rather than desert Him? And in a minute he saw this himself. In the cold, grey dawn outside he heard the cock crow, and just then they were hurrying out the Lord, condemned to death. And as He passed out He gave Peter that one look of unutterable pain that nearly broke poor Peter's heart.

Could Christ ever forgive such a sin? Such sorrow as Peter's will always bring forgiveness. St. Clement tells that Peter never forgot this sin—that whenever he heard a cock crow, he would get out of his bed and cry again to the Lord in shame and tears. See how sweetly the Lord forgave him. Even on the cross and in the Hades world He was thinking of poor Peter. Think of the touching message He left with the angels for the women at the tomb: "Go and tell my disciples *and Peter*—Peter, who has denied Me—Peter, who is breaking his heart, and thinks I have cast him out for ever—tell him especially." Oh, no wonder Peter so fond of Him. No wonder that burst of eager, passionate devotion: "Lord, Thou

knowest all things; Thou knowest that I love Thee!"
(John xxi. 17.)

THE CRUCIFIXION

St. Matthew XXVII. 1-57.

Remember last Lesson. The agony of Gethsemane. Then the arrest. Then that night of weary suffering. What a night it was! The bigotry, and hatred, and malice, and insult from His enemies! The miserable disappointment even from His own disciples. Judas betraying Him; Peter cursing and swearing that he did not know Him; all the rest running away and leaving Him to His fate. What a wretched story!

Then through the night He was hurried from trial to trial, from Annas to Caiaphas—mocked and sneered at for His silence, struck in the face when He ventured to reply, listening to the malicious lying, and twisting, and distorting of His words about the Temple and the tribute. And then came the verdict—the only verdict such a trial could have. What? (xxvi. 66.) They condemned Him as guilty and worthy of death.

§ 1. Judas

We learned in last Lesson of one of the disciples

who was watching all this in awful misery for his sin of denial. Who? Did you ever think that there was probably another disciple watching, too, in still more awful misery for a greater sin? (xxvii. 3.) "When he saw that he was condemned." I suppose he did not expect it. Thought, perhaps, that they would not dare to condemn, or that He, with His Almighty power, would blast them with a look if they touched Him. You can imagine him skulking about the courtyard, keeping out of sight of Peter and John; waiting for news of the trial; hearing the priests, perhaps, ask for himself as a false witness against Jesus, and keeping out of their way or refusing to come forward. Perhaps he saw them buffet Him, and spit on Him, and use Him so shamefully. And then at last he hears to his horror that they have actually gone so far as to condemn Him to death! Poor Judas! he had been fearfully wicked and treacherous; but the remorse of that hour must have been a terrible retribution.

What did he do? (*v.* 3.) Can't you imagine him rushing to the Temple the moment the gates were opened for Morning Service—rushing up to the priests with wild and haggard face: "Take back your money! take back your money! Oh, I have sinned! I have betrayed the innocent blood!"? Can't you imagine the cold sneer of those cruel hypocrites who had no pity on him any more than on his Lord. What was their reply? I think he must have been half-mad at the moment in his terrible remorse. I wonder he did not spring on them and rend them even in that holy place. What did he do? In his rage dashed down the money, ringing and clattering, upon the marble pavement of the Temple, and rushed away madly to hang himself. Oh, wretched Judas! Don't you wish he had rushed up to Calvary instead, and thrown himself for pardon at the foot of the Cross?

§ 2. Pilate

Why did not the priests and scribes put Jesus to death when they had condemned Him? (John xviii. 31.) What did they do? (*v.* 1.) Yes, about six in the morning, as soon as it was safe to rouse the Governor, the mob, with the priests and scribes, and Caiaphas at their head, were clamouring at the gates of the Praetorium; and in the midst of them, pale and worn after the sufferings of the night, and the previous agony of Gethsemane, stood the great, patient Lord, tied with a rope, like a dumb animal for the shambles. "He was led as a sheep to the slaughter." Just think of it: the Almighty Lord and Master of the world waiting there silently in patient, dignified submission to the mad, devilish wickedness of the poor worms He had made; and doing it all for their sake.

Soon the Governor takes his place in the Judgment Hall, ready to judge one of the usual Passover riots, as he thought. What sort of character was Pilate? Strong or weak? Brave or cowardly? He was afraid of the Emperor, and afraid of the mob. Once he had insisted on setting up the Roman standard in Jerusalem, and the mob yelled round his house for six days, till he gave in, and removed the standard. Another time they complained to the Emperor about some golden shields that he had set up; and again, at another time, when he used the money of the Temple Treasury for building a watercourse, the priests and the people made such a disturbance that he was forced to give it back.

So you see his weak indecision made him a wretched judge to have to try a prisoner whom the mob wanted to condemn.

§ 3. *The Trial*

Teacher should read and try to piece together the accounts from the other Gospels. Any "Life of Christ" would help. Trial opens with the question, "What accusation bring ye against this man?" and the reply, "If He were not a malefactor, we would not have delivered Him unto thee." But such vague charges will not do. Must be more definite. Then arises the chorus of complaints: "He perverteth the nation;" "He forbids to pay tribute;" "He says that He Himself is Christ a king!" This is coming to the point which the Governor can understand. So he questions Him directly: "Art Thou the King of the Jews?" and receives the quiet, dignified reply (*v.* 11).

Something in the bearing of the prisoner seems to have impressed Pilate. He evidently did not believe the accusers at all. Why? (*v.* 18.) He knew that bitterness and bigotry would attack any man who ventured to think for himself; and it was clear that the Prisoner before him was of the sort who would not only think for Himself, but would die for His thinking if necessary. Perhaps his Roman training made him feel for a brave man in misfortune. Perhaps there was more than this.

The superstitious fear seemed to grow on him, and this was something more than an ordinary brave man. At any rate, he wants to acquit Him if he can. What does he ask Him? (*v.* 13.) But no answer still. Pilate marvelled greatly. He knows the man is innocent, but he can get no answer from Him.

Then he seems to have taken Him aside in private (John xviii. 33), to ask Him, wonderingly, about this Kingship. "My Kingdom is not of this world," was the calm reply. *"Art* thou a King, then?" "Yes, I am a King; King of all truth-seekers. Everyone that is of the Truth, everyone that wants to follow the highest Right, is my subject."

This is too high a teaching for Pilate, but it certainly is not the teaching of an evil-doer; so he goes out and says to the accusers: "I find no fault in Him." Then arose an uproar that frightened him. "He stirreth up the people from Galilee to Jerusalem!" Pilate eagerly catches at the word "Galilee." It offers him a chance of escape. "Is He from Galilee? King Herod of Galilee is in the city; send Him to him." So he thought to escape responsibility. Did he? No. Herod only sent Him back with one of his old royal robes thrown over Him, to make a mockery of His Kingship. So Pilate had still to judge.

But he is now more troubled than ever. As he took his seat a strange message had come. What? (*v.* 19.) To a superstitious Roman this would be a very evil omen. Pilate would know of the murder of Julius Caesar, and the strange dream of Caesar's wife, which might have saved him if attended to. He is greatly disturbed. How can he escape condemning that "Just Man"? What is his next attempt at escape? (*vv.* 15 to 17.) What result? Ah, Annas and Caiaphas are too clever for that trick. There was nothing else that Pilate could do now, except what a brave, true man would have done at first. What? And Pilate was not capable of that courage. What did he do? (*v.* 14.) Be always ashamed of being a coward, like Pilate. He knew Jesus was innocent. He did not want to condemn Him; but he did not dare to face opposition for sake of doing right. And that want of daring to do right has branded him with eternal shame. The Swiss have a legend that his ghost still walks on Mont Pilatus in the moonlight, always hopelessly washing his hands. No use to wash his hands, or assert innocence of the "blood of this Just Person." Obstinately that blood has clung to him through all the ages since. All over the world to-day, every little child who can say the Creed, repeats, "Suffered under Pontius Pilate."

§ 4. *The Guard-Room*

Now a horrible scene in the barrack-room. The brutal guards get the Prisoner to themselves. Good jest to make fun of Him as King. So, after the horrible scourging, Herod's old purple cloak is thrown over His bleeding shoulders, and they place Him on a raised seat, in mockery for a throne. And they bow the knee before Him, saying, "Hail! King of the Jews." Then the bright idea strikes one of them, and he climbs down into the garden to tear off a bough of sharp-thorned acanthus, and twist it into a wreath, and, amid loud, brutal laughter, the pale, silent King is crowned and sceptred. They thought all this would vex Him and make Him angry. Did it? Could anything make Him angry? Ah! yes. But not anything done to Himself. If they put a stumbling-block before His little ones (St. Matthew xviii. 6); if they injured the helpless, or neglected the needy, that would make Him terribly angry. But the cruel injury to Himself only made Him deeply sorrowful for the men who had fallen so low.

It always irritates cruel people if you seem not to mind their cruelty. So they got angry and violent. (See v. 30.) We can't speak of it—it was unspeakably horrible. But suddenly they got a fright. In the midst of their brutality they looked round, and lo! Pilate, the Governor, has come in, and sees it all. At once the brutal horseplay ceases, and Pilate (I think to move the compassion of the mob) brings forth his pale, brave Prisoner so cruelly outraged. (See John xix. 1-16.) What result? Nothing but a wild outburst of rage from the chief priests and officers. "Crucify Him! Crucify Him!" That was Pilate's last effort, and it failed. "Therefore he delivered Him to be crucified."

§ 5. Calvary

Then the hot, wretched walk to Calvary. Jesus struggling to carry the cross, and fainting under its weight. No wonder after that awful night and morning. Who carried it with Him?

The details of the Crucifixion are very awful, but the

chief impression left on us is the grand, calm patience of the Lord. The brutal soldiers strip Him, and then squabble over the dividing of His clothes, like the relatives of a dead man over the property left behind. He stretches Himself, as directed, on the cross, and the great spikes are driven through His quivering limbs; and then He is lifted up to be exposed to the crowd, and mocked at in His terrible agony. Tell me the three classes of mockers? (*vv.* 39-44.) The passers-by were sneering, "If Thou be the Son of God, come down from the cross!" The cruel priests were gloating over their revenge. They had never forgiven Him for His terrible exposure of them in the Temple, for His words of blame and awful warning. Now was the hour of revenge. Even the two robbers, perhaps two of Barabbas' band, joined in their cruel taunt. What was it? (*v.* 42.) "He saved others, Himself He cannot save." Was it true? Yes. Far more true than they could understand. How? He must choose between Himself and us. If He is to save us, He cannot save Himself. And where Jesus Christ is concerned there can be but one decision in that choice. What? Aye, never did He think of Himself from the cradle to the cross. His whole life was one long self-sacrifice for others. His death must be the same. "I lay down My life for My sheep."

Is it not awful to think that men could treat Him thus? That many to this day are mocking and neglecting Him, giving Him more pain and sorrow? And is it not very touching to think of the sweet, tender patience of Christ? It is just here comes in the first of the "voices from the cross," as He looks on the heathen soldiers and the thoughtless, sinful crowd. He prays not for vengeance on their cruelty, nor for deliverance for Himself. What? (Luke xxiii. 34.) Think of the generous nobleness of such a heart as that. If that nobleness does not subdue our hearts, nothing else will.

I wonder if the mob heard that prayer. I think so, and that God heard it on their behalf. See how they were touched (Luke xxiii. 48). Do you think the robbers heard it, and did God answer it on their behalf? (Luke xxiii. 42.) Did the brutal soldiers? One of them reached up a sponge with wine to relieve His thirst, and their centurion and his fellow-soldiers were so impressed with all they saw and heard (Mark xv. 39; Matthew xxvii. 54). Even for the wicked, bigoted priests, I think, it was heard (Acts vi. 7). Let us think of Christ's prayer, and be thankful for it, and be touched by that tender love and pity, that exquisite unselfishness, that at such a time could forget Himself to pray for others, even for His enemies.

Now comes sixth hour. What o'clock? Darkness lasted until? Dense darkness at noonday. Must have frightened them all. Did they think He would come down from cross, as they mockingly asked? Darkness came as a veil to conceal His awful sufferings. Not merely of body. He could easily bear that. Awful torment of soul. We can't understand it. He knew it was coming on. He sent away His mother, to spare her the sight of it. No human being can ever understand the awful three hours' agony in the darkness on Calvary. He had looked forward to it with dread in the Garden of Gethsemane. We can judge of its awfulness by the awful cry at its close.

What? (*v.* 46.) What a tremendous impression that cry must have made. It is the *only one* of the words on the cross that either St. Matthew or St. Mark record.

We can dimly guess at the meaning of that cry. We are on holy ground at the most solemn point in the sufferings of our Lord. There seems but one way to understand it. That He was the Divine Sin-bearer, bearing the world's sin. "He was wounded for our transgressions, He was bruised," etc. (Isaiah liii. 5). God "made Him to be sin for us, Who knew no sin." The peculiar punishment of sin is the being abandoned by God. In some mysterious way our Lord had to be made to feel that—some sense of utter desolation—something so terrible that even He could hardly endure it. Yet it seemed necessary to the full bearing of our sin. We cannot understand it. But this we can understand, that it was all "for us men and for our salvation."

§ 6. *The End*

And now cometh the end. For all these hours He has been hanging upon the cross in awful conflict. Now, after that cry of agony, the conflict seems over, and the weary soul of the Redeemer turns to Heaven with that title of child-like love, which, through Him, ever since is permitted to us all. "It is finished," He said. "Father, into Thy hands," etc.; and having said thus, He gave up the ghost.

And so the message comes to us from His cross to-day. I want you all to learn it and repeat it after me:

THE CRUCIFIXION

"I gave My life for thee,
  My precious blood I shed,
That thou might'st ransomed be,
  And quickened from the dead.
I gave My life for thee,
What hast thou given for Me?"

LESSON XXIV

THE KING OF GLORY

St. Matthew XXVII. 57 to end, and XXVIII.

§ 1. *Friday Night*

A funeral in a beautiful garden, amid the brightness and perfume of flowers, in the quiet sunset time. Oh! what a miserable funeral! Did ever such hopeless mourners follow a corpse as those who followed the blood-stained body of Jesus to the tomb that evening? Did ever such desolate hearts return from a funeral? It is a terrible dismal thing returning from any funeral—leaving body of loved one in grave—going into empty house—thinking of all the long dreary days of loneliness stretching out in front.

All that here. But far worse. Not only lost the dearest, truest friend but lost all the bright hopes of the future. They had thought He was the Divine Messiah—to redeem Israel—to found the Kingdom of God—to dwell with them always in power and glory. What an awful disappointment and shaking of their trust to see Him arrested, and tried like a common prisoner—helpless in

206

the power of His enemies, mocked, and scourged, and spat upon; nailed upon a cross between two common robbers; taunted to come down, and not doing so; bleeding and weakening, and at last dying like any ordinary man; the pale, blood-stained corpse put into the tomb. Surely there is an end of all—their love, their hopes, their future are all buried in the tomb. He could not be the Christ of God, after all. He must have been mistaken. He was good and pure, and holy. The noblest heart that ever came from God. But He could not have been the Son of God, since death had conquered Him. Thus they went home from that funeral with hearts utterly crushed. Two of them were too heart-broken to go home at all. Who? Think of the two solitary women sitting there alone as the dark night fell on them, in their passionate, despairing grief, in their deep, hopeless love. That is our last view we get of the funeral of Jesus.

§ 2. Saturday

It was the Sabbath day, when people rested from their work and went to church to worship God. Oh! the misery and desolation of that Sabbath! Judas hanged. Peter going wild with remorse; all the rest sunk in hopeless grief; going to church, perhaps; hearing the prayers said by the cruel priests who had murdered their friend; then the men planning sadly to go back to their fishing and tax-gathering, and the women waiting through the night with spices and ointments—for what? Keep body from corruption. How utterly blind to the great joy before them.

I want you to realize all this, that you may realize more fully the glad surprise of the Easter morning.

Now tell me what additional precautions the chief priests and Pharisees were taking on that Sabbath day. They must have been planning it all the time while they were in church (*vv.* 62-66). So the Sabbath evening closed with a strange scene—a guard of soldiers tramping through the quiet garden, the chief priests stretching cords across the opening of the tomb, and sealing them with their signet rings, so that they could tell if tomb tampered with.

§ 3. *Easter Morning*

Read chapter xxviii. Who had been latest at the grave on Friday night? Who first at tomb on the Sunday? Somehow it seems that their love and devotion were deeper than that of the men. I think it is so generally. Perhaps, because women are to be the mothers of the race, and to bring up the little children, God has given them in a very high measure the grace of fidelity and devotion. And the Lord Jesus seems to have had especially the power of drawing it out. In His whole life we never hear of any woman being hostile to Him. Perhaps it was the self-sacrifice in Him that touched and attracted them. Do you think they had more faith and hope than the men? Did they expect the Lord to rise? How do you know they did not? What did they bring to the tomb? Yes; to preserve the body from decay. You see they, too, had lost faith, and lost hope; but what had they not lost? Love. Their love, stronger than death, kept them watching at the tomb after all the others; brought them early to the tomb before all the others. And so the highest honour was given to them. It was a woman who first saw the Lord after He arose. It was women who first received His loving salutation. And ever since, through His influence, the whole position of woman in the world has been changed. Wherever Christianity has power, woman is no longer despised and degraded, as in the olden days, but honoured and treated with chivalrous courtesy, according to the will of Christ.

Now think of the two women walking sorrowfully up the Calvary path to anoint a dead body. And then think of their sudden and awful terror—think of the earthquake shaking the hills—of the burst of terrific glory—of the diamond-shining whiteness of the angel's wings. For I think the women saw it all. St. Matthew uses the word "Behold!" (*v.* 2), as if to suggest the start that it gave them. St. Luke tells of two angels. St. Matthew of but one, perhaps because that one was the speaker. But whether one or two, we may be sure that the sight made the women's hearts beat fast with expectation. Surely, surely, angels would not come but for some great purpose!

How glad the angels must have been to have such joyful news—to be the heralds of the King again. Do you remember first time they were His heralds? Christmas hymn, "Hark! the herald," etc. Perhaps these same two had been in that Christmas chorus at Bethlehem. Don't you think they were glad at Easter? And with no selfish gladness. For they had no fear of death themselves.

But glad for the poor, sorrowful world; and glad, with wondering gladness, for themselves, at the further knowledge of the Divine love.

What was the announcement to women? How did they receive it? Fear and great joy. Too frightened and astonished to grasp the glad news at first. But, oh! what delight as soon as they realized it. Not only their Lord alive, but all their old trust and hope restored. He *was* the Christ, the Son of God, after all. He had not deceived them or been mistaken. All that He had said about heaven and immortality was true—grandly, gloriously true. What a glad, delightful change from the misery of yesterday!

What two helps to belief does the angel give them? (*v.* 6.) (1) "He is risen, *as He said*"— i.e., He first reminds them of the Lord's own words about rising again, which used only to puzzle them, and which now came back to them with new and wonderful meaning. "Of course that is what was meant! It must be true! We see it now!" And then (2) he calls them to come and look for themselves into the empty tomb. "Nobody here, you see." "He is not here. He is risen. Come, see the place," etc. Oh! think of the wild, wondering gladness surging up in their hearts at that moment. And as you think of it, think how that gladness, in calmer form, has flowed down to us through all the centuries since. Every time we stand by an open grave, every time we sit down to cry for the death of one whom we dearly loved, there comes to us the sweet peace of the Resurrection news. We believe that as "Jesus died and rose again, even so them also who sleep in Jesus will God bring with

Him." What would this poor, sad world do to-day if the tomb had remained closed that Easter morning over the dead body of Jesus Christ? What difference would it make to us? (Let the children try to think out the answer for themselves). Then point out that—(1st) We should not be able to believe that He was God, and therefore His glad Gospel would lose most of its value; and (2nd) We should not have much reason to believe that we ourselves should rise again, or the dear ones gone from us; and surely that would make an enormous difference in this sorrowful world.

§ 4. The Easter Missionary Message

When their hearts were so full of the glad news, what directions did they get? (*v. 7.*) What missionary thought does that suggest to us? That the new glad knowledge brought with it a new glad duty to go off at once and make others sharers in the joy. It was a "day of good tidings;" they must not hold their peace.

As they started on their errand what happened? Don't you think they were glad? And as they fall at His feet in loving reverent worship, is there not something about our Missionary Lesson again? Ah! yes. "Go, and tell my brethren." Worship is good. The joy of lying at His feet is good; but better, and more acceptable in His sight, to go off and tell the good news to those who do not yet know it. So the lesson for us, too. Think of the poor heathen who don't know that glad message at all. When their little children die, they do not hope to meet them again. When they are dying themselves, they know nothing of the blessed hereafter, nor of the great love of God, revealed through Jesus Christ. Do you think the Easter news worth having? Is it worth telling? Will some of you pray that, if it be God's will, He will let you go out, when you grow up, to teach the poor heathen the glad message about our Lord? It is so hard to get people to go.

§ 5. *Final Rejection of the King*

Tell me about the priests bribing the soldiers to tell a terrible lie (*vv.* 11-15). A very stupid lie. But it shows, at any rate, that the grave was empty, in spite of their guard of soldiers, and that they were at their wits' end to trump up some explanation. But the sad and terrible thing is that it shows their fierce hatred to Christ, and their awful determination to reject Him at any cost from being their Lord and King. You remember how He prophesied about the husbandmen who should cast the heir out and kill him (*ch.* xxi. 38). They did that. They did worse. When He rose again, and thus proved His Divine claim, they actually concocted a lie to try and keep Him out of His Kingdom. What stupid foolishness! As if anybody's lying and scheming could upset the great plans of God!

Do you remember at His birth somebody else tried by a great sin to keep Him from His Kingdom? (Lesson I) And I told you then that Herod had about as much chance of thwarting God as a little child would have of stopping an express train. So with these chief priests. "The King of the Jews" had been born amongst the Jews, and lived and worked for them, and in return they crucified Him. "Shall I crucify your King?" said Pilate. And He went on, quietly brushing aside their opposition as if they had been so many little cobwebs in His path. He let them crucify Him; He died. And then He calmly rose again to the great Kingship of "all nations."

§ 6. *The King of "All the Nations"*

Now, after our six months of study, we reach the last scene which St. Matthew records in the Lord's life. We began when He was "born King of the Jews" (Lesson I). We thought how the King was crowned, and went forth to battle; how he founded His Kingdom; how He gave them laws for that Kingdom; how He told parables of the Kingdom; how He ordained His followers to proclaim His Kingdom. But always, up to this, there was a peculiar limitation. What? To the Jews only (St. Matthew x. 5, 6). If the Jews had accepted Him, they would have been probably used to convert the world. But they did not. And now He has to turn from them to take His great Kingdom Himself.

This is a most important meeting. Specially appointed by Him before His death. It is the gathering of the little church about its Master—the gathering of the subjects about their King. Probably this is the meeting of which St. Paul tells us, when "He was seen of 500 brethren at once" (1 Corinthians xv. 6). That must have been in Galilee, since in Jerusalem there were only 120 disciples (Acts i. 15); so, probably, it was at this time that the whole crowd was there with the eleven. And then came the great command, What? "All the nations." He who gave that command must surely have been Divine. How else could He send these few ignorant men to take possession of "all the nations" in His name? Fancy a set of ignorant men going to proclaim His name in the mighty Roman Empire, and to all the nations of the earth. How mad it would look if He were not God! But because He was God, there was nothing impossible in it.

Then, after He had given His final command about His "Kingdom of God," He ascended into heaven, and from thence is looking to see how we carry out His command.

So the "Kingdom of God" is going on spreading still. The Church is still going on at His command "making disciples of all the nations." And you and I are members of the Kingdom, and bound to help in the great work of the King. Thus His story closes for the present. No longer do we think of Him as King of the Jews. He is King of "all the nations," of all the universe. "Thou art the King of Glory, O Christ!"